I0235070

Victorian Visions

A Christmas Poetry Collection

Victorian Visions

A Christmas Poetry Collection

Featuring the Poetry of
Emily E. S. Elliott
Katherine Lee Bates
Frances Ridley Havergal
Christiana Georgiana Rossetti
Catherine Winkworth

Compiled and Edited By
Douglas D. Anderson

Lulu, Inc.
Morrisville, North Carolina 27560

Victorian Visions
A Christmas Poetry Collection
Douglas D. Anderson
Copyright © 2007
All Rights Reserved

Cover Artwork: "Regina Angelorum," 1900
William Bouguereau (1825-1905)

The text of this book was set in 12 point Bookman
Old Style; Display used throughout is Arial.

Printed in the United States of America by Lulu, Inc.
Morrisville, North Carolina 27560

ISBN: 978-0-6151-6376-5

Lulu ID 1102962
Hardcover With Dust Jacket:
http://www.lulu.com/content/1102962

Douglas Anderson's Christmas Storefront
http://stores.lulu.com/carols_book

Introduction

That time we call the Victorian era is commonly measured by the 63-year rule of England's longest-reigning monarch, Queen Victoria (reign 1837-1901). It is acknowledged that during this time England saw many cultural and economic changes. In our own day, we can see the vast differences between lyrics and music that was popular in 1940 and that which is popular today.

The five poets in this collection all lived during the reign of Queen Victoria. The eldest of the group, Catherine Winkworth, was born in 1827, and first published in 1855. The youngest, Katherine Bates, was born in 1859, published her last collection in 1926, and lived until 1929 (additional poetry was published posthumously). The span of published poetry by these five was 71 years.

In this collection, we have a wide variety of poetic vision. We have poetry that celebrates Christmas both as holy day and as holiday. The intended audiences of these poems include both children and adults. And we have both English and American poets. Thus, it is hoped, the scope of this collection will allow ample opportunity to celebrate this most favorite season of the year, from Advent through Candlemas.

Many poems have become favorite hymns when a musical setting was created for them. If I've found a public domain setting for a poem in this book, it is indicated by a note that follows the poem (i.e., "See: <u>Carol Name</u>") and the location of the poem at my web site, *The Hymns and Carols of Christmas.*

I've retained the spelling and punctuation as found in the sources. Other errors only are my own, and I am mindful of the advice of William Hone (1823):

> ... I am bound to confess the existence of a few errors ... that were discovered too late for correction, though in sufficient time to enable me to affirm, as a warning to others, that the worst editor of an author's writings is himself.

Some of these poems previous appeared in the following collections, also published by Lulu, Inc.:

- *Once A Lovely Shining Star*
  A Christmas Poetry Collection

- *Father and Daughter*
  Christmas Poems by William Henry Havergal and Frances Ridley Havergal

- *A Holy Heavenly Chime*
  The Christmastide Poems of Christiana Georgina Rossetti

- *All My Heart This Night Rejoices*
  The Christmas Poems of Catherine Winkworth

These books are published in two formats: paperback in the Large Page Format (8 ½ x 11"), and Glossy Hardcover (8 ½" x 11").

Additional poetry, prose, recordings, and a large number of hymns, carols and other songs of the Christmas-tide are also available at my website, *The Hymns and Carols of Christmas*. I hope that you will visit and enjoy the vast fare of Christmas literature available at this site throughout the holiday season.

Douglas D. Anderson
Tigard, Oregon, USA
July 7, 2007

The Hymns and Carols of Christmas
http://www.HymnsAndCarolsOfChristmas.com

This compilation is copyright 2007 by Douglas D. Anderson, and may not be included in any other collection, in any form.

Victorian Visions

Contents

Emily E.S. Elliott
1836-1897

Katherine Ann Bates
1859-1929

Frances Ridley Havergal
1836-1879

Christina Georgina Rossetti
1839-1894
Advent

Catherine Winkworth
1827-1878

Ah! Lord, How Shall I Meet Thee

The Heart Longing for the Inner Advent ("Wherefore dost Thou longer tarry")

Comfort, Comfort Ye My People

Let The Earth Now Praise the Lord

Once He Came In Blessing

The Deliverer ("Arise, the kingdom is at hand")

The Dayspring from on High ("Ye heavens, oh haste your dews to shed")

The New Year ("Thank God that towards eternity")

Thou Virgin Soul!

Wake, Awake, For Night Is Flying

Ye Sons Of Men, In Earnest

Christmas

Christmas Eve:

A Carol ("From heaven above to earth I come")

Christmas Day:

The Word Made Flesh ("O Thou essential Word")

Sunday after Christmas Day:

The Desire of all Nations ("Thee, O Immanuel, We Praise")

A Song of Joy at Dawn ("All my heart this night rejoices")

We Love Him for He First Loved Us ("Thou fairest Child Divine")

Let Us All With Gladsome Voice

God With Us ("Blessed Jesus! This Thy lowly manger is")

Sources

Index of First Lines

Victorian Visions

Emily Elizabeth Steele Elliott

1836-1897

Christmas Poems

Selected From

Chimes of Consecration

London: Seeley, Jackson and Halliday, 1875

Emily Elizabeth Steele Elliott was born at Brighton, England, July 22, 1836, the daughter of the Rev. Edward Bishop Elliott and Harriet Emily Steele.

In addition to *Chimes of Consecration,* Ms. Elliott was also the author of *Chimes for Daily Service,* 1880. This volume contained 71 hymns arranged in two parts, the second of which was published separately as a large-print book for hospitals and infirmaries with the title *Under the Pillow* (see pp. 8-18 below). Many of her hymns were written for the choir at St. Mark's Church, Brighton, England, where her father, Rev. Edward Bishop Elliott, was the rector. Rev. Elliott wrote extensively, including the monumental commentary on The Book of Revelation, *Horæ Apocalypticæ* ("Hours with the Apocalypse"). Ms. Elliott is also said to be the author of the translation "Stilly Night, Holy Night" in 1858, one of the first to appear in English (I have been unable to locate a copy). See: *Silent Night, Holy Night – Notes.*, http://www.hymnsandcarolsofchristmas.com/Hymns and Carols/Notes On Carols/silent night holy night notes .htm

Associated with the Evangelical Party of the Anglican Church (also known as the "Low Church Party"), she spent her life working with rescue missions and children in their Sunday Schools. For six years she edited a magazine titled *Church Missionary Juvenile Instructor*. A number of her poems, some of which were set to music, were published in that magazine.

She was a niece of Charlotte Elliott, author of the hymn, "Just as I Am." Two of Emily's uncles were Evangelical Party ministers, one of whom was Rev. Henry Venn Elliott, author of the hymn "Sun Of My Soul," based on a poem by Rev. John Keble in *The Christian Year*, a copy of which can be found at my web site under the title "Tis gone, that bright and orbed blaze," http://www.hymnsandcarolsofchristmas.com/Hymns and Carols/NonChristmas/tis gon e that bright and orbed b.htm.

Ms. Elliott died at Mildmay, London, August 3, 1897.

Emily E. S. Elliott

A lengthy biography of Charlotte Elliott and an analysis of "Just As I Am" can be found in Louis F. Benson, *Studies of Familiar Hymns, Second Series.* Philadelphia: The Westminster Press, 1923, pp. 194-206.

Sources:

- Louis F. Benson, *Studies of Familiar Hymns, First Series.* Philadelphia: The Westminster Press, 1924.

- Rev. Duncan Campbell, *Hymns and Hymn Makers.* London: A & C. Black, 1908.

- Cyberhymnal: *Emily Elizabeth Steele Elliott,* citing Charles S. Nutter and Wilbur F. Tillett, The *Hymns and Hymn Writers of the Church.* New York: The Methodist Book Concern, 1911.

- John Julian, *Dictionary of Hymnology.* 1892, 1907.

- Robert Guy McCutchan, *Our Hymnody: A Manual of the Methodist Church.* Second Edition. New York: Abingdon Press, 1937.

- Stephen, Leslie, ed., *Dictionary of National Biography.* Vol. XVII. New York: Macmillan and Co., 1889.

Victorian Visions

Emily E. S. Elliott

"Order Thou!"

From Part II. *Chimes Among The Shadows*
Page 35.

WILL the New Year bring greetings
   Blithesome and gay?
Long looked-for meetings,
   Joy's sunny day?
      Father, we know not!
      Coming joys show not:
Hear our entreatings—
   Choose Thou the way!

Will the New Year bring weeping—
   Sorrow's increase?
Will the New Year bring sleeping—
   Quiet release?
      Father most tender,
      We can surrender
All to Thy keeping :—
   Grant us Thy peace!

"That the King of Glory may come in."

From Part I. *Chimes of Consecration*
Pages 24-25.

THOU did'st leave Thy throne and Thy Kingly crown,
   When Thou earnest to earth for me;
But in Bethlehem's home was there found no room
   For Thy Holy Nativity:
O come to my heart, Lord Jesus!
   There is room in my heart for Thee.

Heaven's arches rang when the angels sang,
   Proclaiming Thy Royal degree;
But of lowly birth cam'st Thou, Lord, on earth,
   And in great humility:
O, come to my heart, Lord Jesus!
   There is room in my heart for Thee.

The foxes found rest, and the birds had their nest
   In the shade of the cedar tree;
But Thy couch was the sod, O Thou Son of God,
   In the deserts of Galilee:
O come to my heart, Lord Jesus!
   There is room in my heart for Thee.

Thou earnest, O Lord, with the living word,
  That should set Thy people free;
But with mocking scorn and with crown of thorn
  They bore Thee to Calvary:
O come to my heart, Lord Jesus!
  Thy cross is my only plea.

When Heaven's arches shall ring, and her choirs shall sing
  At Thy coming to victory,
Let Thy voice call me home, saying, "Yet there is room!
  There is room at My side for thee:"
And my heart shall rejoice at the Bridegroom's voice,
  When He cometh and calleth for me.

See:
"Thou Didst Leave Thy Throne."
http://www.hymnsandcarolsofchristmas.com/Hymns
_and_Carols/thou_didst_leave_thy_throne.htm

A Christmas Message

Written for Hospital Distribution

From Part II. *Chimes Among The Shadows*
Pages 68-72.

F AR from home thy Christmas keeping,
    Sad through weariness and pain,
Thou, perchance, hast thought with weeping,
    "Christmas-time has come again !"

Dreams of well-remembered places
    Fill thy memory to-day;
Longing thoughts of loving faces—
    Thoughts of dear ones far away;

Of the little ones who gather
    Round the fire the boughs to weave,
Happy homes where mother, father,
    Keep with them their Christmas Eve;

Of the days when thou wast singing
    Gleeful songs of other times,
While across the fields came ringing
    Far and near the Christmas chimes.

Say'st thou now, "Those joys are over;
    Not for me those home delights;
Dark the clouds that o'er me hover,
    Lone the days and long the nights?

Emily E. S. Elliott

Chiming bells and happy voices
   Fall but sadly on my ear;
All the world without rejoices;
   They are glad—while I am here."

Are these thy words, oh, mourner?
   Are these thy thoughts, my friend?
Then listen now to a message
   Which home to thy heart we send,

In words which the wind came bringing
   From the hush of a quiet room,
Where voices were softly singing
   In the twilight's gathering gloom.

And so sweet and clear was the music
   Of the message tender and true,
That now in the Christmas season
   We would sing it forth to you

The "Fear not" of Christmas-tide

From Part II. *Chimes Among The Shadows*
Page 62.

M OURNER, Christmas comes for thee;
    Hear, with low and gentle tone,
One who whispers, "Look to Me!
    Hope, for thou art not alone!"

Not for thee the merry throng,
    Gladness making lonelier still;
Yet is thine the angels' song,
    Echoed clear from Bethlehem's hill.

"Fear ye not!" from heav'n was spoken
    Long ago, on Christmas Eve;
"Fear thou not!" is still the token
    Which our waiting hearts receive.

"Unto you the Christ is given!"
    Thus sang choirs full and clear;
Now a voice on Christmas Even
    Softly echoes, "He is here!"

He knows all—thy Lord divine,
    Mourner, though thine eye be dim,
Look to Christ;—His love is thine;
    Take thy Christmas joy from Him.

Emily E. S. Elliott

Song of Christmas

From Part II. *Chimes Among The Shadows*
Page 69.

IS there gladness in the house?
  Now lift your song once more;
For Christ, the new-born King,
Doth joy and gladness bring,
And His people praise and sing,
  And joyfully adore!

Is there weeping in the house?
  Oh weary, weep no more!
For you shines Christmas morn,
And Jesus Christ was born
To comfort those who mourn
  On sorrow's lonely shore.

Is there scarceness in the house?
  Yet rise in hope once more!
For Christ, the Lord on high,
Who at Christmas time came nigh,
Is listéning to thy cry,
  And He Himself was poor.

Is there stillness in the house?
  A shadow on the floor?
Are there voices hushed and low
Where the mourners come and go?
Oh listen! ye shall know
  Christ, who wept, is at the door.

Now let our songs arise;
   And let our hearts adore;
For e'en in sorrow's hours,
In sunshine and in showers,
The Christmas joy is ours,
   Abiding evermore!

Thus, my sister, thus, my brother,
   We to thee would comfort send,
Softly whisp'ring of Another—
   Of a nearer, better Friend.

He who at this season holy
   Came to earth thy grief to heal,
Led a sorrowing life and lowly;
   He hath suffered—He can heal.

Dost thou weep to be forgiven?
   From thy load of sins set free?
He, the Lord of earth and heaven,
   Bore their chastisement for thee.

Dost thou sigh through ceaseless tossing
   On a couch whence sleep has fled;
Grief and pain thy future crossing—
   Thine a wearied, aching head?

He has said, who once was weary,
   "Lean thy head upon My breast;
Life for Me was lone and dreary,
   I know all—yet bring thee rest.

Emily E. S. Elliott

"I know all; I stand beside thee;
    On My heart thy burden lay;
Safe beneath My wings I hide thee,
    Keep with thee thy Christmas Day.

"Trust Me! I will never leave thee;
    Love Me! for I love thee well;
Whisper forth the thoughts that grieve thee,
    Fear not sin and care to tell.

"Christmas bells for thee are ringing,
    Christ, thy Lord, to thee draws near;
Angels hymns for thee are singing,
    Fear thou not: thy King is here!

"Though thy tear-dimmed eyes be holden;
    Though My form thou canst not see:
I, who dwell in glory golden—
    I, the Lord, am close to thee!"

*   *   *   *   *   *

Therefore smile amidst thy weeping;
    Therefore hope through all thy fears;
Therefore let thy Christmas-keeping
    Bring thee sunshine through thy tears:

Cast on Jesus all thy sorrow,
    On His strength thy weakness stay;
Trust Him for a brighter morrow,
    Keep with Him thy Christmas Day!

The Old Year and the New.

From Part II. *Chimes Among The Shadows*
Pages 78-79.

HUSH! the year is dying,
    Soft, without a sound;
Snow-flakes, shroud-like, lying
    On the earth around:
All its strivings over,
    All its story done;

*   *   *   *   *   *

Now—its mem'ries hover
    O'er a year begun.

Some of us were lonely
    In its brightest hours;
Sadly whispering, "Only
    Let Thy will be ours!"
Some of us were tired
    In its summer days:
Weary, we desired
    Gladder, brighter ways.

Emily E. S. Elliott

We but seemed repeating
    Changeless rounds of life,
Daily, hourly meeting
    Well-known cares and strife.
Life a little colder,
    Fewer loving faces,
We but growing older
    In familiar places.

Now the year is over,
    Let us braver stand,
Seeking to discover
    His—our Father's—hand:
Let us "follow wholly,"
    Though our sight be dim:
He would make us holy
    For a life with Him.

Every day He sends us
    He Himself prepares;
He Himself attends us
    Through its joys and cares;
His true love beseeching,
    Let us, then, draw near;
Seeking guidance, teaching,
    For the op'ning year.

" The Watchman said, 'The Morning cometh.' "

From Part II. *Chimes Among The Shadows*
Pages 80-82.

W ATCHMAN, what of the night?
　　The earth is dark and cold:
And but faint is the starry light
　Which our waiting eyes behold.
Will the morning never come,
　　With its beacons in the sky,
To dissipate the gloom
　　Ere the Bridegroom shall draw nigh?
　　　Watchman, what of the night?

"Oh, slumber not nor sleep,
　Though the night be dark and long;
But your solemn vigils keep
　Through the Church's even-song:
Arise, and watch, and pray,
　For we see the light afar
That heralds in the day
　Of the bright and morning star:
　　Watch and pray!"

Emily E. S. Elliott

We have pray'd and waited on
    For our absent King's return;
But the hours have come and gone,
    And our tapers dimly burn:
Still dark is the midnight sky,
    There are enemies abroad,
And we hear the heathen cry
    Saying, "Where is now their God?"
        Watchman, what of the night?

"O watching and waiting band,
    Now lift ye your heads on high,
For the morning is near at hand,
    And the Bridegroom is drawing nigh.
When the tapers are burning dim
    We know that the night is o'er;
And the chant of the morning hymn
    Shall echo from shore to shore:
        Watch and pray!"

We have wash'd our garments white
    From the stains of an evil world,
And we wait for the sun in his might,
    And the banner of God unfurl'd.
We are looking to Zion's hill,
    And we know that the day is near;
But we watch for the summons still,
    And the voice that we long to hear.
        Watchman, what of the night?

"There are banners of red and gold,
    Far out in the shining east;
The curtains of night are uproll'd
    For the morn of the marriage-feast.
Still wait for the Bridegroom's voice,
    Then go ye forth to meet Him;
Let the hearts of His saints rejoice
    As they lift their song to greet Him:
        Watch and pray!"

Emily E. S. Elliott

New Year's Eve

From Part III. *Chimes From Heather-Bells; And Others*
Page 122

WITH echoing chime, in the midnight time,
    The good old year will end;
And with earnest care and with loving prayer,
    I think of thee, my friend.

Thine be joy in the year before thee,
    Thine be love from thy loved ones round;
Hope's glad sunlight stream brightly o'er thee,
    Best and calm in thy home abound!

Be it thine in the year beginning,
    Grief to lessen—to lighten care;
Thine to shine on the sad and sinning
    With loving deeds, and with earnest prayer;

Thine to know, amid shades descending,
    One, whose presence shines bright and clear
Thine a gladness that knows no ending,—
    The changeless joy of a changeless year.

Thus I think of thee, thus I pray for thee,
    Now at the old year's end:
Heaven's blessing light up thy way for thee!
    I wish thee joy, my friend.

The Yule-log

From Part III. *Chimes From Heather-Bells; And Others*
Pages 115-116.

WE have gathered the logs for the Christmas fire;
    Where are the children to bring them in?
Pile them steadily, higher and higher!
    Here is the youngest! let him begin!
Not a finer Yule-log burns in all the shire
    Than this, which the woodman has toiled to win.

Christmas was glorious in England olden:
    So they tell us in ancient rhymes;
Let us make the age that we live in golden
    For days to come live out "good old times:"
Our hist'ries, Heav'n's message to Earth unfolden,
    Our gladness an echo of Christmas chimes.

Let us throw on the flames of our kindling fire
    Harsh remembrance and thought of feud;
Vengeful feeling, self-will'd desire,
    All that was bitter and coarse and rude;
And now, while the blaze rises higher and higher;
    Let our Christmas hearth be a holy rood!

Emily E. S. Elliott

Let us warm our hearts while we warm our fingers,
    Peace and goodwill holding gentle thrall;
While the Angels' psalm on our memory lingers
    Let kindly words tell of love to all.
Open the door to the carol singers!
    Let the Bethlehem hymn sound from hearth and
hail.

Thou hast no frown for us, cold December!
    Care and trouble aside we leave;
Golden the light of each glowing ember,
    While our voices we blend, and glad hopes we
weave:
And for absent friends, whom we all remember,
    Let us breathe a prayer on this Christmas Eve!

The Child Jesus

From Part IV. *Chimes Of Child-Land*
Pages 125-126.

THERE came a little Child to earth
  Long ago:
And the angels of God proclaimed His birth,
  High and low.
Out on the night so calm and still
  Their song was heard,
For they knew that the Child on Bethlehem's hill
  Was Christ the Lord.

* * * * * *

Far away in a goodly land,
  Fair and bright,
Children with crowns of glory stand,
  Robed in white;
In white more pure than the spotless snow,
  And their tongues unite
In the psalm which the angels sang long ago
  On Christmas night.

They sing how the Lord of that world so fair
    A Child was born,
And that they might a crown of glory wear,
    Wore a crown of thorn:
And in mortal weakness, in want, and pain,
    Came forth to die,
That the children of earth might for ever reign
    With Him on high.

He has put on his Kingly apparel now,
    In that goodly land:
And He leads to where fountains of water flow
    That chosen band:
And for evermore, in their garments fair
    And undefil'd,
Those ransom'd children His praise declare
    Who was once a Child.

See:

"There Came A Little Child To Earth - Version 1"
http://www.hymnsandcarolsofchristmas.com/Hymns
 and Carols/there came a little child to ear.htm

"There Came A Little Child To Earth - Version 2"
http://www.hymnsandcarolsofchristmas.com/Hymns
 and Carols/there came a little child to 2.htm

"Lord, what wilt Thou have Me to Do?"

From Part IV. *Chimes Of Child-Land*
Pages 127-130

I.

O COULD I have been in the Holy Land
 When our dear Lord Christ was there,
Could I have been one of the chosen band
 Appointed His path to share,
My chief delight both by day and by night
 Had been for His wants to care.

I could not have flown, upon angel's wings
 His ministry to fulfil;
I could not have brought Him costly things;
 But with reverent heart, and still,
I would daily have stored each sacred word
 Declaring the Master's will.

And I might have sought through the fields of corn
 For the ripest and richest grain;
He would not have looked on my gift with scorn,
 Nor have spurned it with cold disdain;
But He would have smiled on the eager child
 Whose offering was not in vain.

Or I would have journeyed with willing feet
  To the hills of the trailing vine,
And the richest clusters, purple and sweet,
  Would have brought to their Lord and mine,—
In words repeating their lowly greeting,
  "The fruits of the earth are Thine!"

And oh, if my Lord had been passing near
  In the glare of the noon-tide heat,
With cool well-water, sparkling and clear,
  I had waited His steps to meet;
And with loving word, saying, "Drink, my Lord,"
  Would have knelt at the Saviour's feet.

But the earth was orphaned when Jesus went;
  I wish we could see Him here!
Or at least that a message to me were sent,
  That an angel might once appear,
Who with gracious speech would appoint to each
  Some work for the Master here!

II.

A message has come from the Holy Land,
  From the King who once dwelt below,
A message for all who obedient stand,
  And are waiting to serve Him now;
O Christ our Lord, speak Thou the word,
  Be it ours Thy will to know!

Page 25

Victorian Visions

"I am walking still on the distant earth
   Where I once had my sad abode :
Not in easy paths, not in scenes of mirth,
   Not in pleasure's ensnaring road,
But in lonely ways and through weary days,
   Still wanders the Son of God.

"Men pass me by and they know me not,
   Though their welcome I still implore
In many a dreary and desolate spot
   By the voice of the sad and poor:
Who will not hear when their feet draw near
   Is turning Christ from the door.

"Speak loving words by the lowly bed
   Of her who in sorrow lies;
With tender hand raise the drooping head
   And bring light into tearful eyes;
Still the Master needs such gentle deeds,
   And such lowly sacrifice.

"The bread of life to the weary soul
   The Saviour still bids thee break;
And living water which maketh whole
   To the thirsty in spirit take:
Such offerings meet lie at Jesu's feet,
   When given for His dear sake.

"From thee let the tidings spread abroad
    Of the love which brings sinners nigh;
That He who once bow'd 'neath our sorrow's load
    Still heals as He passes by;
That life is given, and hope and Heaven,
    To all who for mercy cry.

"Thus do His will while thy path still lies
    Through the earth which He trod for thee,—
For a little while, till thy waking eyes
    Shall the King in his beauty see;
And the glad sweet word be in glory heard
    ' Thou hast done it unto Me! ' "

New Year's Morning

From Part IV. _Chimes Of Child-Land_
Pages 131-134.

W E made our plan by the fire's red light,
　　As we sat on the hearth-rug, Janie and I;
We wanted so much to sit up last night,
　　To sit up, and to see the old year die.

We thought how much we should like to hear
　　If the clock sounded just as at other times,
And to wish each other a Happy New Year
　　As the last stroke died of the midnight chimes.

But they all of them shook their heads, and said,
　　How long we should both of us have to wait;
And that birds in their nests go so soon to bed,
　　And how cross we should grow if we sat up late.

Yet, once we stayed up until half-past ten,
　　When we went to the feast at the harvest-home;
We haven't been much more cross since then,
　　And it's very seldom that New Years come.

But we couldn't get them to give us leave,
　　Though they let us stay until nearly nine;
And then—the last thing on our New Year's eve—
　　We peeped out to see if the night was fine.

Emily E. S. Elliott

We waited until we were left alone,
    And then in the darkness we raised the blind;
To have wakened and found the old year gone
    Without one good-bye, would have been unkind.

It seemed to us that the world outside
    Had never before been so full of sighing—
As if down the valley, and far and wide,
    Everything knew that the year was dying.

Round the church, from across the meadows,
    The wind was sounding like burial marches;
And where house-lights glimmered the muffled shadows
    Seemed stealing past towards the old grey arches.

And two stars like funeral tapers shone
    Through the clouds which had gathered across the sky;
Heavy cloud-blinds which would be let down,
    We said, when the good old year should die.

Then we promised each other to lie awake,
    And we tried very hard the watch to keep
But Janie's eyes would grow heavy, and ache,
    And at last we both of us fell asleep.

And now, and now it is New Year's day,
    And the snow has fallen all white and glistening,
Over the meadows and far away,
    A spotless robe for the New Year's christening.

Victorian Visions

Have angels or fairies been here by night,
  To where earth and leaves were all brown and
sodden?
I want Janie to wake and look out at the sight,
  At the pure white glitter of snow untrodden.

Untrodden now !—o'er the meadows hoary,
  Soon many feet will pass to and fro:
At the end of the day we shall read its story
  In foot-prints left on the spotless snow.

Every one who comes through the garden,
  Must leave his track on the path to-day;
A track which the clear sharp frost will harden,
  Till the sun shall have melted the ice away.

I think I am glad,—it seems almost right
  That things this morning should happen so—
That the world without should be hung in white,
  And not a foot-print have marked the snow.

I suppose they would call it a childish dreaming,
  Which grown-up people can't stay to hear,
But the things outside in the world are seeming
  Like a picture to me of the opening year.

I mean, that it seems as if like the snow,
  An unwritten page were before us spreading;
The year is new and unsullied now—
  The path which we all shall so soon be treading.

Emily E. S. Elliott

A path in which each of us leaves a track,
  In which foot-prints of children's feet remain;
A path over which we can't travel back,
  For old years never are new again.

I think that the months pass so very slowly,
  Though one's parents say that they fly too fast:
I wish I could keep this New Year holy,
  Better by far than I kept the last!

I can't, without Him for my one true Guide,
  Whose face the children in heav'n behold:
Where the snow is untrodden, the path untried,
  He, only, aright can my steps uphold.

He can make me walk as His loving child,
  He can teach me to work for Him here below;
And oh, when my ways have been sin-defil'd,
  He Himself can wash me whiter than snow.

Janie, I've been the first to waken,
  And oh! such beautiful things are here! —
The mists and darkness their flight have taken,
  And I want to wish you a Happy New Year.

Wake up, Janie, and see the sight!
  Wake up, Janie, and look at the snow!
The good old year died at twelve last night,
  It's a happy New Year to us, Janie, now!

November

From Part IV. *Chimes Of Child-Land*
Pages 157-158

THE winter is coming! the children cry,
    And are thinking of frozen fingers:
"Only here and there do the red leaves lie
    While the beautiful autumn lingers;
The days are growing so short and drear,
    And it's cold getting up in the morning;
We wish that the summer were always here,
    Our gardens and fields adorning!"

The wind passes over the field forlorn
    And sighs out its tale of trouble:
"I once was a field of golden corn,
    And now I'm a field of stubble!"
The birds have flown to the sunny South,
    And the Robin is grave and steady,
As if not caring to open his mouth
    Till his Christmas songs are ready.

Cheer up, children! behind the bars
    The fire glows in the twilight;
A few more weeks, and the Christmas stars
    Will be winking down through the skylight:
There's a message for all of us,—you and me,
    In this brown and gray November;
There's work for which we must all agree
    Ere the twenty-fifth of December.

Emily E. S. Elliott

See, bright are the garlands November weaves,
    For the year so quickly dying;
Let us gather up crimson and golden leaves
    Which here on the ground are lying:
Let us gather up many an earnest thought
    Which we had when the year was younger;
Shall we let them wither and come to nought,
    Or, living them, make them stronger,

And wreathe them now in the autumn drear,
    My little sisters and brothers,
Into deeds which shall gladden the fading year,
    Into gentle care for others?
There are many whose sorrows our love may lighten,
    The lonely, the sad, the weary;
And those who for others the way would brighten
    Will not find the winter dreary.

Christmas

From Part IV. *Chimes Of Child-Land*
Pages 159-160.

E CHO forth the Christmas carol,
    Now the holly garland weave;
Deck the church with green apparel,
    In the light of Christmas Eve.
        For Christmas comes with a song,
            And with words of holy cheer;
        With children's laughter in happy throng,
            And with hopes for a glad New Year!

Brighten, with the Christmas greeting,
    Eyes through pain and weeping dim:
To the sad in heart repeating
    Echoes of the angels' hymn.
        For their Christmas comes with a sigh,
            And with thoughts of other times;
        And many a dream of the past floats by
            With the sound of the midnight chimes.

Think of those who still are ours,
    Though in regions far away;
Sunny skies and starry flowers
    They would give for home to-day:
        For their Christmas comes where they roam
            With a thought of over the sea;
        And with tender dreams of the friends at home,
            And a soft—"Will they think of me ?"

Now, while friend with friend is meeting,
  While the glistering boughs they wreathe,
Send I forth for thee my greeting,—
  Loving prayers for thee I breathe:
    May thy Christmas come with a song,
      With the light of the Christmas Star;
    May visions bright o'er thy pathway throng,
      And joys from a Land afar!
    Such hopes for thee I weave,
      While the bells chime full and clear;
    And oh, may the light of thy Christmas Eve
      Shine soft o'er a glad New Year!

Here Ends

The Christmas Poems
Of
Emily E. S. Elliott

Victorian Visions

Katherine Lee Bates

1859 – 1929

Christmas Poems

Selected From

Fairy Gold

New York: E. P. Dutton & Co., 1916

America The Beautiful And Other Poems

New York: Thomas Y. Crowell Company, 1911.

And

Other Sources As Noted

B orn on Aug. 12, 1859, Katherine Lee Bates was the fifth child born to William and Cornelia

Frances Lee Bates. The family had come to Falmouth, Mass. in 1858. The Rev. Bates served as pastor of the First Congregational Church on the Village Green.

As noted in church records, Katharine was baptized on September 4, 1859, when she was only three weeks old. Because of his illness, her father was unable to travel to the church. A friend, Rev. Professor Butler of Madison University came to the Bates' home to officiate at Katharine's baptism. Her father died six days later, on September 10. "Katie" was said to have eased the pain of her mother's first years of widowhood.

At age 12, life in Falmouth ended when the family moved to Granitville, now known as Wellesley Hills. She attended Wellesley High School, graduating in 1874. In 1878, She graduated from the more advanced Newton High School. Bates then entered Wellesley College, graduating with a Bachelor of Arts degree in 1880. She became president of it's second graduating class and returned to teach for 40 years.

She also studied at Oxford, England, and earned a master's degree in arts from Wellesley College. Over the years, Bates took four year-long sabbaticals to travel – three of which were abroad – plus numerous shorter voyages. Countries she visited included England, Ireland, Scotland, Switzerland, France, Spain, Egypt, Palestine, and Norway. In 1916, she would be awarded the degree of Doctor of Literature from Oberlin College. A second honorary degree would be conferred, and a third from Wellesley in 1925 upon her retirement: Doctor of Laws. She had been a teacher for 45 years, one who had inspired immense affection and respect, both personally and professionally.

The author of 32 books and a large number of articles, Dr. Bates was well-traveled, gracious, witty, popular, and scholarly without being pretentious. Falmouth remained her home town, revisited nearly every year.

Katherine Lee Bates was the first known writer to introduce Mrs. Santa Claus to the American scene in the book *Goody Santa Claus on a Sleigh Ride*, published in 1889 ("Goody" was a common contraction of the day for "goodwife"). It was during that year that she had suffered from the grippe (an old term for influenza) and was on convalescent leave. During that time, she wrote a large amount of children's literature and poetry. She spent 1889-1890 at Oxford. Returning, she felt that as a full professor, she should not concern herself with juvenile literature any more. The sequel to her earlier *Rose and Thorn* (1889) was abandoned. For some time, she devoted her efforts to more serious writing of articles and books, while continuing to write a large amount of poetry.

By 1909, however, her position had softened, and she again included children's literature among her output. Later, she would write other poems for children about Christmas, included in *Fairy Gold* (New York: E. P. Dutton & Co., 1916), which also included "Goody Santa Claus."

At the summit of Pike's Peak, Colorado in 1893 the opening lines of "America the Beautiful" floated into her mind, and gave new meaning to the spectacular view. A sculptor has portrayed the young poet at that moment. "America the Beautiful" first appeared in print in *The Congregationalist*, a weekly journal, on July 4, 1895. Professor of English Literature at Wellesley College, Dr. Bates lectured that summer at Colorado College, Colorado Springs.

She rewrote some sections, and the new version was published In *The Boston Evening Transcript* on Nov. 19, 1904. Perhaps the most intense criticisms centered on the word "beautiful," which some called hackneyed. But Bates refused to change that word, for she claimed it best described America. Following the 1904 publication, part of the third stanza was altered, thereafter, the poem was unchanged; Bates retained the copyright, protecting it from misprints and deliberate changes.

She remained at Wellesley until she retired as chair of the English department in 1925. In her journal, she quoted G. K. Chesterton's lines:

> Lo! I am come to autumn
> Where all the leaves are gold.

In 1926, her last volume of poetry was published (in her lifetime): *The Pilgrim Ship*. In those final years, her life became more leisurely, more casual, and more intimate. She was still sought out by many, including the New England Poetry Club and the National Hymn Society. She continued to write, and upon request, review the works of others (described as "keen and gentle"). Her last collection of verses, *America the Dream*, was published after her death.

She died early in the morning of March 28, 1929, at the age of 70, listening to the words of Whittier's *At Last*, read to her by her friend, Mrs. Guild. At Wellesley, the flag at Tower Court was lowered, and then raised to half-staff. After her death, a chair of English literature was endowed in her name. In her obituary, printed in Wellesley's *The Townsman*, Mr. Bradford wrote:

> The death of Katharine Lee Bates means the passing away of one of the most notable citizens of Wellesley, one of the most important figures connected with Wellesley College, and much more than that, a considerable author and creative influence in the whole of American life.

Her ashes were buried beside her parents and her sister in Falmouth's Oak Grove Cemetery. A statue of Dr. Bates was erected in front of the Falmouth Public Library; photographs of Bates are also available at that same site, and at a page of the web site at Wellesley College.

Source:

Dorothy Burgess, *Dream and Deed: The Story of Katharine Lee Bates* (Norman: University of Oklahoma Press, 1952).

Victorian Visions

Christmas Island

Source: Katherine Lee Bates, *Fairy Gold.*
New York: E. P. Dutton & Co., 1916.

Fringed with coral, floored with lava,
Three-score leagues to south of Java,
So is Christmas Island charted
By geographers blind-hearted,
— Just a dot, by their dull notion,
On the burning Indian Ocean;
Merely a refreshment station
For the birds in long migration;
Its pomegranates, custard-apples
That the dancing sunshine dapples,
Cocoanuts with milky hollows
Only feast wing-weary swallows,
Or the tropic fowl there dwelling.
Don't believe a word they're telling.
Christmas Island, though it seem land,
Is a floating bit of dreamland.
Gone adrift from childhood, planted
By the winds with seeds enchanted,
Seeds of candied plum and cherry:
Here the Christmas Saints make merry.

Victorian Visions

Even saints must have vacation;
So they chose from all creation,
As a change from iceberg castles
Hung with snow in loops and tassels,
Christmas Island for a summer
Residence. The earliest comer
Is our own saint, none diviner,
Santa Claus. His ocean-liner
Is a sleigh that's scudding fast.
Mistletoe climbs up the mast,
And the sail, so full of caper,
Is of tissue wrapping-paper.
As he steers, he hums a carol,
But instead of fur apparel
Smudged with soot, he's spick and spandy
In white linen, dear old dandy,
With a Borealis sash on,
And a palmleaf hat in fashion
Wreathed about with holly berry.
Welcome, Santa! Rest you merry!

Next, his chubby legs bestriding
Such a Yule-log, who comes riding
Overseas, the feast to dish up,
But — aha! — the boy's own bishop,
Good St. Nicholas! and listen!"
Out of Denmark old Jule-nissen,
Kindly goblin, bend, rheumatic,
In the milk-bowl set up attic
For his Christmas cheer, comes bobbing
Through the waves. He'll be hob-nobbing
With Knecht Clobes, Dutchman true,
Sailing in a wooden shoe.
When the sunset gold enamels
All the sea, three cloudy camels
Bear the Kings with stately paces,
Taking island for oases,
While a star-boar brings Kriss Kringle.
Singing *Noël* as they mingle,
Drinking toasts in sunshine sherry,
How the Christmas Saints make merry!

Victorian Visions

While a gray contralto pigeon
Coos that loving is religion,
How they laugh and how they rollick,
How they fill the isle with frolic.
Up the Christmas Trees they clamber,
Lighting candles rose and amber,
Till the sudden moonbeams glisten.
Then all kneel but old Jule-nissen,
Who, a heathen elf stiff-jointed,
Dofts his nightcap, red and pointed;
For within the moon's pale luster
They behold bright figures cluster;
Their adoring eyes look on a
Silver-throned serene Madonna,
With the Christ-Child, rosy sweeting,
Smiling to their loyal greeting.
Would that on this Holy Night
We might share such blissful sight,
— We might find a fairy ferry
To that isle where saints make merry!

Katherine Lee Bates

Santa Claus' Riddle

Source: Katherine Lee Bates, *Fairy Gold*.
New York: E. P. Dutton & Co., 1916.

Of all the happy and holy times
That fill the steeples with merry chimes
And warm our hearts in the coldest climes,
'Twas Christmas eve, as I live by rhymes.

One by one had the drowsy oaks
Wrapt about them their snow-flake cloaks,
And snugly fastened, with diamond pins,
Fleecy nightcaps beneath their chins.

The stars had kissed the hills good-night,
But lingered yet, with a taper light,
Till the chattering lips of the little streams
Were sealed with frost for their winter dreams.

And the silver moonbeams softly fell
On cots as white as the lily-bell,
Where the nested children sweetly slept,
While watch above them their angels kept.

Eyes of gray and of hazel hue,
Roguish black eyes and bonny blue,
All with their satin curtains drawn,
Peeped not once till the shining dawn.

Victorian Visions

But still through the silent eventide
Brown eyes twain were opened wide,
Where, bolt upright in his pillows, sate
A wise little wean called Curly Pate.

Now yet the lore of schools and books
Had troubled the peace of his childish looks,
But through the valleys of Fairyland
He had walked with Wisdom, hand in hand.

Once midsummer eves he would hear, perchance,
The shrill, sweet pipes of the elfin dance,
And their dewy prints in the dawning trace
On tremulous carpets of cobweb lace.

He had caught the clink of the hammers fine,
Where the goblins delve in their darksome mine,
In green cocked hats of a queer design,
With crystal tears in their ruby eyne.

He had seen where the golden basket swings
At the tip of the rainbow's dazzling wings,
Full of the silver spoons that fall
Into the mouths of babies small.

He had met Jack Frost in tippet and furs,
Pricking his thumbs on the chestnut burrs,
And this learnèd laddie could tell, no doubt,
Why nuts fall down and friends fall out.

And now, while the dusky night waxed late,
All nid-nodding sat Curly Pate,
Scaring the dreams, whose wings of gauze
Would veil his vision from Santa Claus.

And ever he raised, by a resolute frown,
The heavy lids that came stealing down
To rest their silken fringes brown
On the rosiest cheek in Baby-Town.

Till at last, — so the legend tells, —
He heard the tinkle of silver bells;
Tinkle! tinkle! a jocund tune
Between the snow and the sinking moon.

O, then, how the heart of our hero beat!
How it throbbed in time to the music sweet,
While gaily rung on the frosted roofs
The frolicsome tramp of reindeer hoofs!

And down the chimney by swift degrees
Came worsted stockings and velvet knees,
Till from furry cap unto booted feet
Dear Saint Nicholas stood complete.

Blessings upon him! and how he shook
His plumb little sides with a mirthful look,
As he crammed, his bright, blue eyes a-twinkle,
The bairnie's sock in its every wrinkle.

May he live forever — the blithe old soul,
With cheeks so ruddy and shape so droll,
Throned on a Yule-log, crowned with holly,
The king of kindness, the friend of folly!

His task was done, and he brushed the snow
From his crispy beard, as he turned to go;
From his crispy beard and his tresses hoar,
As he tiptoed over the moonlight floor.

But the sparkling flakes to delicious crumbs
Of frosted cakes and to sugar-plums
Changed as they fell, whereas near by
A bubble of laughter proved the spy.

Back from the chimney flashed the Saint,
And stamped his feet in a rage so quaint
That from scores of pockets the dolls in flee
Popped up their curious heads to see.

"Oho!" in a terrible voice he spake,
"By the Mistletoe Bough! a boy awake!
Now freeze my whiskers! but in my pack
I'll stow him away for a jumping-jack.

"Wise as an owlet? Quick! the proof!
My reindeer stamp on the snowy roof.
So read my riddle, if sage you be,
Or up the chimney you go with me.

"Name me the tree of the deepest roots,
Whose boughs are laden with sweetest fruits,
In bleakest weather which blooms aright,
And buds and bears in a single night."

Did Curly Pate tremble? Never a whit.
Below the curls was the mother-wit;
And well I ween that his two eyes brown
Spied the dimple beneath the frown.

So shaking shyly, with childish grace,
The ringlets soft from his winsome face,
He peeped through his lashes and answered true,
As I trow that a brave little man should do:

"Please thy Saintship, no eyes have seen
Thy wondrous orchards of evergreen;
But where is the wean who doth no long
The whole year through for thy harvest song?

"The *Christmas Tree* hath struck deep roots
In human hearts: its wintry fruits
Are sweet with love, And the bairns believe
It buddeth and beareth on Holy Eve."

A stir in the chimney, a crackle of frost,
A tinkle of bells on the midnight lost;
And in mirth and music the riddling guest
Had smiled and vanished, as saints know best.

But low on his pillow the laddie dear
Sank and slumbered, till chanticleer,
Crowing apace, bade children wake
To bless the dawn for the Christ-child's sake.

Note:

This poem also appeared in her *Sunshine And Other Verses For Children*, 1890.

Santa's Stocking

Source: Katherine Lee Bates, *Fairy Gold.*
New York: E. P. Dutton & Co., 1916.

Dame Snow has been knitting all day
  With needles of crystal and pearl
To make a big, beautiful stocking
For Santa, her merriest son;
And now in some wonderful way
She has hung it, by twist and by twirl,
On the tip of the moon, and sits rocking,
Old mother, her day's work done.

How long and how empty it flaps,
Like a new, white cloud in the sky!
The stars gleam above it for candles;
But who is to fill it and trim?
Dame Snow in her rocking-chair naps.
When Santa comes home by and by,
Will he find — O scandal of scandals! —
No Christmas at all for him?

Katherine Lee Bates

Dear Saint of the reindeer sleigh,
At his tink-a-link-tinkle-a-link,
The evergreens blossom with tapers;
'Tis Christmas by all the clocks;
And wherever he calls, they say,
The most polished andirons wink,
The sulkiest chimney capers,
And Baby kicks off its socks.

His pack is bursting with toys;
The dollies cling round his neck;
And sleds come slithering after
As he takes the roofs at a run.
Blithe lover of girls and boys,
Bonbons he pours by the peck;
Holidays, revels and laughter,
Feasting and frolic and fun.

Who would dream that his kind heart aches
— Heart shaped like a candied pear,
Sweet heart of our housetop rover —
For the homes where no carols resound,
For the little child that wakes
To a hearth all cold and bare,
For Santa, his white world over,
Finds Christmas doesn't go round!

Dame Snow has been knitting all day
With needles of crystal and pearl
To make a big, beautiful stocking
For Santa, her busiest son;
And now in some wonderful way
She has hung it, by twist and by twirl,
On the tip of the moon, and sits rocking,
Old mother, her day's work done.

Victorian Visions

Let us bring the dear Saint from our store
Fair gifts wrapped softly in love;
Let all gentle children come flocking,
Glad children whose Christmas is sure;
Let us bring him more treasures and more,
While the star-candles glisten above,
For whatever we put in his stocking,
Santa Claus gives to the poor.

Lolita's Bethlehem

Source: Katherine Lee Bates, *Fairy Gold.*
New York: E. P. Dutton & Co., 1916.

Seven shining sunsets
   Lead to Holy Night,
And Lolita's Bethlehem
   Grows with her delight.
Lola, Lolita,
   Little Spanish lass!
Blithly for Lolita
   The seven sunsets pass.

Under Moorish arches
   Trips a timid tread.
First we give the Holy Child
   With the haloed head,
And demure Lolita
   Makes her small salaam,
Cherishing the Baby
   In a roseleaf palm.

Victorian Visions

Blue and gold the sunset
    On our second eve;
A Madonna blue and gold
    Lifted hands receive;
And Lolita scampers,
    With a shout of joy,
To carry Mary Mother
    "To her little boy."

Frolic of light footsteps
    Dancing to the door;
Who is waiting on a staff,
    Figure bowed and hoar?
Merrily Lolita,
    Black eyes mischievous,
Kisses old Saint Joseph
    Before she kisses us.

It is not Lolita,
    Sweetheart, who will scorn
For her Holy Family
    Cow with crumpled horn.
Lola, Lolita,
    Hugs it close and vows
That it is her darling,
    The caramel of cows.

Seven shining sunsets,
    One by one they pass.
From a pearly twilight comes
    Humble Brother Ass.
Lovingly Lolita
    Teaches him his part:
"Kneel beside St. Joseph,
    Donkey of my heart."

Next a china shepherd
  With two curly sheep,
But Lolita hushes them
  Ere she lets them peep
At the Christ-Child, shedding
  Tenderness and awe,
Where He slumbers softly
  On a wisp of straw.

Last of seven sunsets!
  Hardly can we wait
For Christmas Eve to enter in
  By that gleaming gate;
While Lolita's angel,
  Balanced on a star,
Acrobat with lilac wings,
  Plays a pink guitar.

Blissfully Lolita,
  Careful not to hurt,
Gathers all the images
  In her little skirt.
Lola! Lolita!
  To bed she carries them,
For to-night all childhood
  Sleeps in Bethlehem.

Goody Santa Claus

Source: Katherine Lee Bates, *Fairy Gold.*
New York: E. P. Dutton & Co., 1916.

S anta, must I tease in vain, Dear?
    Let me go and hold the reindeer,
While you clamber down the chimneys.
    Don't look savage as a Turk!
Why should you have all the glory
    of the joyous Christmas story,
    And poor little Goody Santa Claus
    have nothing but the work?

It would be so very cozy,
    you and I, all round and rosy,
Looking like two loving snowballs
    in our fuzzy Arctic furs,
Tucked in warm and snug together,
    whisking through the winter weather
Where the tinkle of the sleigh-bells
    is the only sound that stirs.

You just sit here and grow chubby
    off the goodies in my cubby
From December to December,
    till your white beard sweeps your knees;
For you must allow, my Goodman,
    that you're but a lazy woodman
And rely on me to foster
    all our fruitful Christmas trees.

While your Saintship waxes holy,
    year by year, and roly-poly,
Blessed by all the lads and lassies
    in the limits of the land,
While your toes at home you're toasting,
    then poor Goody must go posting
Out to plant and prune and garner,
    where our fir-tree forests stand.

Oh! but when the toil is sorest
    how I love our fir-tree forest,
Heart of light and heart of beauty
    in the Northland cold and dim,
All with gifts and candles laden
    to delight a boy or maiden,
And its dark-green branches ever
    murmuring the Christmas hymn!

Yet ask young Jack Frost, our neighbor,
    who but Goody has the labor,
Feeding roots with milk and honey
    that the bonbons may be sweet!
Who but Goody knows the reason
    why the playthings bloom in season
And the ripened toys and trinkets
    rattle gaily to her feet!

Victorian Visions

From the time the dollies budded,
    wiry-boned and saw-dust blooded,
With their waxen eyelids winking
    when the wind the tree-tops plied,
Have I rested for a minute,
    until now your pack has in it
All the bright, abundant harvest
    of the merry Christmastide?

Santa, wouldn't it be pleasant
    to surprise me with a present?
And this ride behind the reindeer
    is the boon your Goody begs;
Think how hard my extra work is,
    tending the Thanksgiving turkeys
And our flocks of rainbow chickens —
    those that lay the Easter eggs.

Home to womankind is suited?
    Nonsense, Goodman! Let our fruited
Orchards answer for the value
    of a woman out-of-doors.
Why then bid me chase the thunder,
    while the roof you're safely under,
All to fashion fire-crackers
    with the lighting in their cores?

See! I've fetched my snow-flake bonnet,
    with the sunrise ribbons on it;
I've not worn it since we fled
    from Fairyland our wedding day;
How we sped through iceberg porches
    with the Northern Lights for torches!
You were young and slender, Santa,
    and we had this very sleigh.

Jump in quick then? That's my bonny.
    Hey down derry! Nonny nonny!
  While I tie your fur cap closer,
    I will kiss your ruddy chin.
I'm so pleased I fall to singing,
    just as sleigh-bells take to ringing!
  Are the cloud-spun lap-robes ready?
    Tirra-lirra! Tuck me in.

Off across the starlight Norland,
    where no plant adorns the moorland
  Save the ruby-berried holly
    and the frolic mistletoe!
Oh, but this is Christmas revel!
    Off across the frosted level
  Where the reindeers' hoofs strike sparkles
    from the crispy, crackling snow!

There's the Man i' the Moon before us,
    bound to lead the Christmas chorus
  With the music of the sky-waves
    rippling round his silver shell —
Glimmering boat that leans and tarries
    with the weight of dreams she carries
  To the cots of happy children.
    Gentle sailor, steer her well!

Now we pass through dusky portals
    to the drowsy land of mortals;
  Snow-enfolded, silent cities
    stretch about us dim and far.
Oh! how sound the world is sleeping,
    midnight watch no shepherd keeping,
  Though an angel-face shines gladly
    down from every golden star.

Victorian Visions

Here's a roof. I'll hold the reindeer.
        I suppose this weather-vane, Dear,
    Some one set here just on purpose
        for our teams to fasten to.
There's its gilded cock, — the gaby! —
    wants to crow and tell the baby
We are come. Be careful, Santa!
        Don't get smothered in the flue.

Back so soon? No chimney-swallow
        dives but where his mate can follow.
    Bend your cold ear, Sweetheart Santa,
        down to catch my whisper faint:
Would it be so very shocking
        if your Goody filled a stocking
Just for once? Oh, dear! Forgive me.
        Frowns do not become a Saint.

I will peep in at the skylights,
        where the moon sheds tender twilights
    Equally down silken chambers
        and down attics bare and bleak.
Let me show with hailstone candies
        these two dreaming boys — the dandies
In their frilled and fluted nighties,
        rosy cheek to rosy cheek!

What! No gift for this poor garret?
        Take a sunset sash and wear it
O'er the rags, my pale-faced lassie,
        till thy father smiles again.
He's a poet, but — oh, cruel!
        he has neither light nor fuel.
Here's a fallen star to write by,
        and a music-box of rain.

So our sprightly reindeer clamber,
    with their fairy sleigh of amber,
On from roof to roof, the woven
    shades of night about us drawn.
On from roof to roof we twinkle,
    all the silver bells a-tinkle,
Till blooms in yonder blessèd East
    the rose of Christmas dawn.

Now the pack is fairly rifled,
    and poor Santa's well-nigh stifled;
Yet you would not let your Goody
    fill a single baby-sock;
Yes, I know the task takes brain, Dear.
    I can only hold the reindeer,
And so see me climb down chimney —
    it would give your nerves a shock.

Wait! There's yet a tiny fellow,
    smiling lips and curls so yellow
You would think a truant sunbeam
    played in them all night. He spins
Giant tops, a flies kites higher
    than the gold cathedral spire
In his dreams — the orphan bairnie,
    trustful little Tatterkins.

Santa, don't pass by the urchin!
    Shake the pack, and deeply search in
All your pockets. There is always
    one toy more. I told you so.
Up again? Why, what's the trouble?
    On your eyelash winks the bubble
Mortals call a tear, I fancy.
    Holes in stocking, heel and toe?

Victorian Visions

Goodman, though your speech is crusty
    now and then there's nothing rusty
In your heart. A child's least sorrow
    makes your wet eyes glisten, too;
But I'll mend that sock so nearly
    it shall hold your gifts completely.
Take the reins and let me show you
    what a woman's wit can do.

Puff! I'm up again, my Deary,
    flushed a bit and somewhat weary,
With my wedding snow-flake bonnet
    worse for many a sooty knock;
But be glad you let me wheedle,
    since, an icicle for needle,
Threaded with the last pale moonbeam,
    I have darned the laddie's sock.

Then I tucked a paint-box in it
    ('twas no easy task to win it
From the Artist of the Autumn Leaves)
    and frost-fruits white and sweet,
With the toys your pocket misses —
    oh! and kisses upon kisses
To cherish safe from evil paths
    the motherless small feet.

Chirrup! chirrup! There's a patter
    of soft footsteps and a clatter
Of child voices. Speed it, reindeer,
    up the sparkling Arctic Hill!
Merry Christmas, little people!
    Joy-bells ring in every steeple,
And Goody's gladdest of the glad.
    I've had my own sweet will.

Note:

This is one of the first known appearances of "Mrs. Santa Claus." The poem was published separately in 1889 under the title _Goody Santa Claus on a Sleigh Ride_, just when Dr. Bates abandoned the writing of children's verse (which she resumed, fortunately, in 1907).

This poem also appeared in her _Sunshine And Other Verses For Children_, 1890.

Another early poem is "Mrs. Santa Claus" by Charles Henry Lueders (1858-1891). See: Harrison S. Morris, ed., _In The Yule-Log Glow_, Vol. IV. Philadelphia: J. B. Lippincott Company, 1900. Project Gutenberg EBook #20956. Caution: this is a rather "dark" poem; I would not recommend it to children.

The Star Of Bethlehem

Source: Katherine Lee Bates, *America The Beautiful And Other Poems.* New York: Thomas Y. Crowell Company, 1911, pp. 93-94.

S OFTLY I come into the dance of the spheres,
  Into the choir of lights,
      New from my nest in God's heart.
  O Night, the chosen of nights,
Longing and dream of the years,
      Blessèd thou art.

Golden the fruit hangs on the hyaline tree;
    Golden the glistening tide
        Sweeps through the heavens; the cars
    Of the great mooned planets glide
Golden; and jet to me
        Bow down the stars;

Casting their crowns, bright with aeonian reigns,
    Under the flight of my feet
        Eager for Bethlehem,
    Thither with music-beat
Blent of innumerous strains
        Marshalling them.

Sweetly their chant soars through unsearchable
  space,
      Quivering vespers that thrill
          Into the deep nocturne,
      Symphony I fulfill,
I who like Mary's face
          Wonder and yearn,

Cherish, adore, keeping the watch above
      The Word made flesh to-night,
          Wonderful Word impearled
      In childhood holy-white,
Word that is Godhood, Love,
          Light of the World.

Note:

Also found in Martha Foote Crow, ed., *Christ In The Poetry Of Today.* New York: The Womans Press, 1917, pp. 15-16.

_____

The Kings Of The East

Source: Katherine Lee Bates, *America The Beautiful And Other Poems*. New York: Thomas Y. Crowell Company, 1911, p. 95.

I

THE Kings of the East are riding
   To-night to Bethlehem.
The sunset glows dividing,
The Kings of the East are riding;
A star their journey guiding,
      Gleaming with gold and gem
The Kings of the East are riding
   To-night to Bethlehem.

II

To a strange sweet harp of Zion
      The starry host troops forth;
The golden-glaived Orion
To a strange sweet harp of Zion;
The Archer and the Lion,
      The Watcher of the North;
To a strange sweet harp of Zion
      The starry host troops forth.

III

There beams above a manger
    The child-face of a star;
Amid the stars a stranger,
It beams above a manger;
What means this ether-ranger
    To pause where poor folk are?
There beams above a manger
    The child-face of a star.

Note:

Also found in Dorothy Middlebrook Shipman, ed., *Stardust & Holly*. New York: The Macmillan Co., 1933, pp. 79-80.

Also found in Martha Foote Crow, ed., *Christ In The Poetry Of Today*. New York: The Womans Press, 1917, pp. 16-17.

This hymn was written prior to 1911 according to Mrs. George Sargent Burgess, niece of Miss Bates. The editor of many editions of classic texts in American and English literature, the author of seventeen books, Dr. Bates published her first poems in 1887. She was a full professor from 1891 through her retirement in 1925.

The tune "Wallace" was written for this poem for the *Wellesley Song Book*, 1914, by Clarence Grant Hamilton, Mus. Doc. (1865-1935). He was Professor of Music at Wellesley College, as well as organist at the Congregational Church. Among his other books, his *Outlines of Music History*, 1908, is an authoritative work.

Source: Robert Guy McCutchan, *Our Hymnody*. Second Edition. New York: Abingdon Press, 1937, pp. 136-7.

On Christmas Eve

Source: Katherine Lee Bates, *America The Beautiful And Other Poems*. New York: Thomas Y. Crowell Company, 1911, p. 93.

ON Christmas Eve, so runs the marvellous tale,
Heaven once flashed
    through her amethystine veil,
And while this raptured earth beheld and heard
Those star-eclipsing choirs, the Eternal Word
Put on our flesh to bear our human bale.

Faint with the sweets such sanctities exhale,
Deep-brooding Doubt lets fall his winnowing flail,
And feels his weary heart divinely stirred
    On Christmas Eve.

For sudden lustres play o'er hill and dale,
The silence thrills to music, mothers pale
Smile like Madonnas, and the Christ, unblurred
By mists of time, unslain, unsepulchred,
Life's cup re-consecrates to Holy Grail
    On Christmas Eve.

Note:

Also found in Martha Foote Crow, ed., *Christ In The Poetry Of Today*. New York: The Womans Press, 1917, pp. 173-174.

Another Year

Source: Katherine Lee Bates, *America The Beautiful And Other Poems*. New York: Thomas Y. Crowell Company, 1911, pp. 106-107.

E ARTH giveth unto us
Another year
Miraculous
Her beauty to behold,
New dawns of rose and gold,
New starlights to enfold
Our dreaming sphere.

Love giveth unto us
Another year
Of marvellous
Ointments for weary feet,
A shadow from the heat,
Home welcomes and hearth-sweet
Communion dear.

Christ giveth unto us
Another year
Of burdenous
Tasks blessed for His sake,
World's pity to awake,
To bind up hearts that break
Beside us here.

Hope giveth unto us
Another year
Adventurous
To follow the climbing Good,
By thorn and beast withstood,
To heights of brotherhood,
Through dim to clear.

God giveth unto us
Another year
All luminous
With Him, our shining Source,
Divine, redeeming Force,
Of life's bewildered course
Still charioteer.

Winter

Source: Katherine Lee Bates, *America The Beautiful
And Other Poems*. New York: Thomas Y. Crowell
Company, 1911, pp. 142-143.

A HA! he is here again.
His stormy trumpets blow;
The swift, dim lines of the beating rain
Blossom to starry snow,

Till the air is white as a nun
With the whirling, thistledown grace
Of myriad flakes, and every one
A fret of fairy lace.

Each naked stem they cloak
Till it shines like a birch in spring,
And each dry leaf that clings to the oak
Becomes a feathery wing.

With morning the drifts are deep,
And strangely over them go,
Like dreams on the silent heart of sleep,
Shadows of jay and crow;

But the hungry chickadees wait,
Their tree-hollow sealed with ice,
Till the sun shall open that crystal gate
To a sparkling paradise;

For never a branch so bare,
So gnarled and crooked and gray,
But it dazzles with diamonds unaware
And rainbows out at play.

Too soon the sun unfurls
Gold banners in the west;
The diamond pendants pale to pearls,
The flying shadows rest;

And the fair young moon in joy
Comes flushing up the sky,
To find our world a Christmas toy
Carven in ivory.

The New Year

Source: Katherine Lee Bates, *America The Beautiful And Other Poems*. New York: Thomas Y. Crowell Company, 1911, pp. 143-145.

L ONG foretold by those prophets old,
    The sun, the moon, and the stars,
The New Year waits at Time's high gates,
    And clashes the golden bars.

And the soul of the world awakens and gropes
In a twilight wonder of fears and hopes,
As a new wave breaks on the beaten shores,
As a new foot falls on the trodden floors,
And a New Year stands with uplifted hands
    In the light of the opened doors.

    All uncrowned, with his hair unbound,
    His white hair loose on the wind,
    The Old Year goes to his long repose,
      But he casts his gifts behind.
With glimmer of tears and flicker of smile,
He takes his place in the pilgrim file
Of the dim-eyed years who journey along,
Shrilling us back a discordant song,
That mingles and blends with the distance and ends
    In a harmony soft and strong.

Long foretold, in the morning cold,
With pain and music and mirth,
The New Year gleams on the broken dreams
Of the fast-revolving earth;
A secret, a change, and a mystery,
What hath not been and what is to be,
Nourished and cherished and hidden away,
Saved by Time for this ripening day,
To work a deed forever decreed
And a mission it must obey.

All unknown, it is thou alone
Who canst tell thine errand aright,—
A whispered thought when the world was not,
And a sign made in the night.
Far from the touch of our vain surmise,
In thy folded hours thy meaning lies,
To some for blessing, to some for curse;
Yet none would thy destined dawn disperse,
For it works in the plan that is more than man,
And is well for the universe.

The Changing Road

Source: Katherine Lee Bates, *America The Beautiful
And Other Poems*. New York: Thomas Y. Crowell
Company, 1911, pp. 145-146.

B ENEATH the softly falling snow
        The wood whose shy anemones
We plucked such little while ago
        Becomes a wood of Christmas trees.

Our paths of rustling silken grass
        Will soon be ermine bands of white
Spotted with tiny steps that pass
        On silent errands in the night.

The river will be locked in hush
        But frosted like a fairy lawn
With knots of crystal flowers that flush
        By moonlight, blanching in the dawn.

Flown are our minstrels, golden-wing
        And rosy-breast and ruby-throat,
But all the pines are murmuring
        A sweet, orchestral under-note.

So trustfully our hands we lay
        Within the old, kind hands of Time,
Who holds on his mysterious way
        From rime to bloom, from bloom to rime,

And lets us run beside his knee
    O'er rough and smooth, and touch his load,
And play we bear the burden, we,
    And revel in the changing road,

Till ivory dawn and purple noon
    And dove-grey eve have one by one
Traced on the skies their ancient rune,
    And all our little strength is done.

Then Time shall lift a starry torch
    In signal to his gentle Twin
Who, stooping from a shining porch,
    Gathers the drowsy children in.

I wonder if, through that strange sleep
    Unstirred by clock or silver chime,
Our dreams will not the cadence keep
    Of those unresting feet of Time,

And follow on his beauteous path
    From snow to flowers, from flowers to snow,
And marvel what high charge he hath,
    Whither the fearless footsteps go.

Christmas Carols

Source: Katherine Lee Bates, *America The Beautiful And Other Poems*. New York: Thomas Y. Crowell Company, 1911, pp. 276-283.

1

THE Holy Night is flowing by;
    Before the Christmas morn,
Before the stars have left the sky,
    The Christ-Child will be born.

2

When the Eternal a child would be,
    Lovingly he to an angel spoke:
"Gabriel, go to Galilee,
    And in Galilee find the country-folk.
Ask for the village of Nazareth,
    And enter softly, with folded wing,
A little cottage where flourisheth
    The stock of David, my harper-king.
There sits a maiden, poor of dress,
    Espoused to a humble carpenter.
For her purity and her gentleness
    Out of the world have I chosen her."
The wings of the angel drank the air
    Until to that humble home he came,

And Mary marvelled to see him there,
    With wand of lily and plumes of flame.
The bright archangel bowed his knee:
    "Hail, among women most highly blest !
The Lord our God hath chosen thee,
    And Christ shall nestle on thy breast."

3

A group of weary travellers pass
    On the road to Bethlehem,
A maiden mounted on an ass,
    An old man guiding them.
"We must make haste.   The evenings are
    So cold, your clothes so thin,
And poor folk often journey far
    Before they find an inn.
But here one stands.   Halloo! Halloo!
    Inn-keeper, open quick,
For Mary can no further go.
    She's tired and she's sick."
A one-eyed face, all angry-browed,
    Came peering through the gate.
"Who is it calling here so loud,
    And at an hour so late?"
" 'Tis I," returned the troubled saint.
    "A lodging I entreat
For Mary, so forspent and faint
    Her pulses hardly beat."
"Let old St. Joseph go his ways,"
    That inn-keeper replied.
"The good guest is the guest that pays.
    The rest may stay outside."

"Nay, take us in, though I confess
    An empty purse I bear,
But poverty and weariness
    Are sacred everywhere."
"The only sacred thing I see
    Is money. Poor folk may
Lodge where they can, but as for me,
    I kiss the hands that pay."
The one-eyed face drew back, the gate
    Was slammed,—and then went blind
The other eye, to match the state
    Of that benighted mind.
A dog now leads him through the streets,
    Where woefully he sells
Rosaries and ballad-sheets,
    Charms and cockle-shells.

4

The Virgin is spreading handkerchiefs
    On the rosemary to dry.
The little birds are singing,
    And the brook is running by.
The Virgin washes handkerchiefs,
    And spreads them in the sun,
But St. Joseph, out of mischief,
    Has stolen every one.
And then her poor mantillas
    The Virgin washes well.
St. Joseph spreads them in the sun.
    Behold a miracle!
The cloth cuts up itself and makes
    A set of baby-clothes,

So joyful with St. Joseph
  The Virgin homeward goes.

5

Into the porch of Bethlehem
  Have crept the gypsies wild,
And they have stolen the swaddling clothes
  Of the new-born Holy Child.

Oh, those swarthy gypsies!
  What wont the rascals dare?
They have not left the Christ-Child
  A single shred to wear.

6

The night is cold,
  But garlands weave,
And sing the songs
  Of Christmas Eve.
The Child is born.
  Through frosty weather
Kings and shepherds
  Haste together.
Where might such guest
  A welcome win?
Where ox and mule
  Keep the inn.
For bed they give him
  Straw and hay,
The earliest gifts
  Of Christmas Day.

Ox and mule,
    He smiles on them,
The Little Child
    Of Bethlehem.
A Little Child?
    The Prince of Peace,
Whose victories
    Shall never cease.

7

There has been born in a stable,
    Amid the shavings curled,
Between the mule and the ox,
    The Saviour of the world.

And King Melchior said:
" Blow the pipe and sound the horn.
Tell the world that Christ is born."

O Child, with only straw
    To cover Thee from the cold,
Thou shouldst be clad in velvet,
    In velvet and in gold.

Sun, moon and star are shining
    Within that lowly stall,
St. Joseph and St. Mary
    And the Child, most bright of all.

Fire-bells are ringing, ringing
    In Bethlehem to-night.
Tis a star has fallen from heaven
    And set the straw alight.

" Oh, I am a poor gypsy
    Who've trudged o'er field and fell
To bring unto the Baby
    This crested cockerel."

" I am a poor Galician,
    Long roads my feet have hurt,
But here I bring some linen
    To make a baby-shirt."

All bring the Christ-Child presents;
    The poorest does his part;
And I, who am so little,
    Give to Him my heart.

8

Joy, joy, joy!
On the breast of Mary lies a Baby-Boy.
Peace on earth!
At the solemn midnight she gave the Christ-Child
  birth.
Tender one!
In the dark and in the frost is Thy life begun.
Cherubs peep
Through the stable chinks to see their little God
  asleep
In the hay,
Dancing on the roof above Him softly as they may.

Shepherds keep
In the winter pastures watch about their sheep.
In the skies
Suddenly a glorious star astonishes their eyes.
Sore afraid
Stand the shepherds till an angel all in white arrayed
Speaks to them,
While the glory of the Lord is poured on Bethlehem.
" Lo, I bring
Tidings of great joy, the birth of Jesus Christ,
  your King.

You shall find
In a manger, wrapped in swaddling clothes, the
  Saviour of mankind."
Eagerly
The shepherds run to Bethlehem, this miracle to see,
And behold
A stable-door where angels watch with wings of
  shining gold.

Poorly clad
Is the Baby in a petticoat, the best that Mary had.
At her feet
Angels kneel, adoring her, Madonna pure and sweet.
By her stands
Good St. Joseph, serving her with labor-roughened
  hands,
While the kine
With grave and gentle eyes look on at the scene
  divine.
With good leave
Come the shepherds and from all a welcoming smile
  receive ;

Then before
The Virgin bright they bow themselves upon the
  stable floor.
    " Queen," they say,
" Can it be that God Most High puts on mortal clay?
    Mystery!
Thou, the Mother of the Christ, ever blessed be!
    Baby dear,
Do not cry.   It burns our hearts, every little tear.
    Fare thee well,
Father Joseph; thee, our Lady; Thee, Immanuel.
    Had we gold
It were yours, but yours our cots and the sheep we
  fold.
    One more peep
At the Baby. Little One, snuggle down and sleep.
    Señor Mule,
Señor Ox, good-bye to you. Wish you merry Yule!"
    Thus depart
The shepherds with all courtesy, exceeding glad of
  heart.

Christmas Carol

Source: Katherine Lee Bates, *Sunshine And Other Verses For Children.* "Printed By The Wellesley Alumæ for the Benefit of the Norumbega Fund 1890," pp. 67-68.

Calmly the Syrian starlights glisten
    Far on the valleys and mountain-bars.
Why do the shepherds rouse and listen ?
    Stirs an anthem among the stars ?

Joyous melodies thrill and quiver.
    All the air is with music rife,
Sweet as the flow of the crystal river
    Under the shade of the Tree of Life.

Swells the song till the night is holden
    Rapt in gladness and awe and love ;
Splendors amethyst, rose and golden,
    Shed from an arch of wings above.

Soft as a silver mist retreating
    Soar and vanish the seraph throng,
Rainbow plumes still earthward beating
    Fainting strains of the far-off song.

Fade, bright wings, on the purple even !
Wane, oh glory, from hill and mere !
Hence that beautiful song of Heaven
   Earth shall sing, while the angels hear.

The Lame Shepherd

Source: Dorothy Middlebrook Shipman, ed., *Stardust & Holly*. New York: The Macmillan Co., 1933, pp. 65-66.

Slowly I followed on,
Stumbling and falling.
All the air sparkled;
All the air sung.
Even to my dull heart
Glory was calling;
Slowly I followed on,
Stumbling and falling.

Great wings arched over me,
Purple and amber;
Night was all color,
Night was all gleam.
Wearily up the hill
Needs must I clamber,
Though wings arched over me,
Purple and amber.

Proudly the chorus pealed
While I was panting.
Winds were all music,
Voices all praise;
Brooks, birds, the waving trees
Joined in the chanting;
Proudly the chorus pealed,
While I was panting.

Late came my aching feet,
Late to the manger;
All slept in silence,
All dreamed in dusk;
Under the same dear stars,
No star a stranger,
Late came my aching feet,
Late to the manger.

Kissing a baby's hand,
Painfully kneeling,
Sweet little drowsy hand,
Honey of heaven,
Swift through my twisted limbs
Glowed a glad healing,
Kissing a baby's hand,
Kissing and kneeling.

To The Old Year

Source: Katherine Lee Bates, *America The Beautiful And Other Poems*. New York: Thomas Y. Crowell Company, 1911, p. 143.

*A*UF *wiederschen!* For we shall meet before
The throne of God. The drifting snows confuse
   Thy foot-prints. Down the echoing wind I lose
Thy voice. So be it. We shall meet once more.

When from the grave of Time thou com'st again
   To front my soul in Judgment, witness bear
   To error, failure, sin; but oh, my prayer,
My strife forget thou not! *Auf weiderschen!*

Katherine Lee Bates

Christmas After War

Source: Dorothy Middlebrook Shipman, ed., *Stardust & Holly*. New York: The Macmillan Co., 1933, p. 204.

Shall misery make mirth,
    Lord of our disbelief?
What gift of joy has earth?
    Bring me your grief.

How shall old fables heal
    Our world of woe and sin?
*When you through fable feel
    The truth within.*

There is no guiding star:
    The heavens are black and blind.
*The magi journeyed far;
    So must mankind.*

What singing angels press
    Bright wings down these wild skies?
*Courage and faithfulness
    And sacrifice.*

Madonna, Child, are we
    Shepherds to seek for themselves'
*Love ! Peace ! Let your heart be
    Their Bethlehem.*

To Heavy Hearts

Source: Katherine Lee Bates, *The Retinue And Other Poems.* New York: E. P. Dutton & Co., 1918, pp. 59-61.

Heavy hearts, your jubilee
Droops about the Christmas Tree.
Sudden sighs cut off the laughter,
For a haunting pain comes after
All your gallant glee,
—Pain for your soldiers far away to-night,
(O cloud that darkens on the Christmas star!)
Sons, husbands, those who wreathed your world with light,
Far, far, so far.
Be comforted! They never were so near.
In life's deep center of self-sacrifice
You meet with vision clear.
There in love's purest paradise
The touch of soul on soul is close and dear.

Not to-night shall soft cheeks glow
Where the Druid mistletoe
Weaves its charm, while hollies twinkle;
For the lads in some grim wrinkle
Of the earth crouch low.
Hard is their Christmas in the aching trench,
Or in the listening darkness mounting guard,
Haggard with cold and sick with creeping stench,
—Hard, hard, so hard.
Be comforted!   That hardness is their pride.
Salute the strength that can endure the stress
Of such a Christmastide.
Our earth made beautiful shall bless
Their stern young manhood nobly testified.

Silver chimes are on the air,
Sweet and blithe—too blithe to bear;
And what singing hearth rejoices,
Missing the beloved voices
That were merriest there?
The booming cannon are their Christmas bells;
(O Holy Child, how many a homeless waif!)
Their carols are the hiss and crash of shells.
God keep them safe!
Be comforted!   For safe they are within
His quiet hand, your soldiers who fulfil
In steadfast discipline,
Like those calm stars, His patient will
That is the peace beneath all battle-din.

New Year

Source: Katherine Lee Bates, *The Retinue And Other Poems*. New York: E. P. Dutton & Co., 1918, pp. 135-136.

White year, white year,
Muffled soft in snow,
A diamond spray whose gems are gone
Before their grace we know,
A crystal-coated spray whose hours
Melt when looked upon,
Hoarfrost stars and hoarfrost flowers,
        White year !

Green year, green year,
Sweet with sun and showers,
A windblown spray whose blossoms bright
Are the seven-colored hours,
A dancing spray whose leaves are days,
A spray whose leaves delight
In azure gleam and silver haze,
        Green year !

New Year, new year
From rosy leaf to gold,
A shining spray on the Tree of Time
Where myriad sprays unfold,
A spray so fair that God may see
And gather it, bloom and rime,
To deck the doors of Eternity,
     New Year !

Our First War-Christmas

Source: Katherine Lee Bates, *The Retinue And Other Poems*. New York: E. P. Dutton & Co., 1918, pp. 58-59.

Hard to wait for the postman's tramp
Up the snowy walk, for the hand that gropes
Deep in his pack, while the children tease
For the rainbow-ribboned packages,
And women wax faint with their fearful hopes
For those tattered, grimy envelopes
With the foreign stamp,
—Word, dear word from overseas,
From the fleet, the trench, the camp.

Oh, not jewels nor curious toys
Of art and fashion, no gift most rare
Can gladden those eyes that weep in the hush
Of lonely nights, can bring the flush
To faces white with their silent prayer,
Like the letters, precious beyond compare,
From our soldier-boys,
　Letters to laugh over, cry over, crush
To the lips, our Christmas joys.

Here Ends

The Christmas Poems
Of
Katherine Lee Bates

Victorian Visions

Frances Ridley Havergal

1836-1879

Christmas Poems

Selected From

The Poetical Works of Frances Ridley Havergal.

Maria V. G. Havergal, ed.

Toronto: Toronto Williard Tract Depot, ND, circa 1880

The daughter of Rev. William Henry and Jane Head Havergal, Frances was born at Astley, Worcestershire, December 14, 1836, the youngest of six children. Five years later, her father was transferred to the Rectory of St. Nicholas, Worcester. In August, 1850, she entered Mrs. Teed's school, whose influence over her was most beneficial. In the following year, she says "I committed my soul to the Saviour, and earth and heaven seemed brighter from that moment."

Following her education with Mrs. Teed, she took a short sojourn in Germany, and on her return she was confirmed in Worcester Cathedral, July 17, 1853. In 1860, she left Worcester when her father resigned from St. Nicholas, and she thereafter resided in Leamington and at Caswall Bay, Swansea, broken by visits to Switzerland, Scotland, and North Wales. She died at Caswall Bay, June 3, 1879 at the age of 43.

Her scholastic acquirements were extensive, embracing several modern languages, together with Greek and Hebrew. Julian did not regard her as a prominent poet, but he adds that "by her distinct individuality, she carved out a niche which she alone could fill." Julian goes on to write that "simply and sweetly, she sang the love of God and His way of salvation. To this end, her entire life was consecrated."

However, her importance as a poet should not be underestimated. Julian noted that some 70 of her 100 hymns were in common usage at the beginning of the 20th century. But it should be emphasized that these 100 hymns were only a fraction of her output as a poet. In a letter written to David Chalkley of the Havergal Trust, the Rev. Iain H. Murray wrote: "Frances Ridley Havergal was one of the most gifted poets ever to write for the Christian church. To this day some of her hymns are sung and loved all over the world yet much of her no-less valuable writing and poetry has long been scarce and little known." (October 31, 2003)

Her religious views and theological bias are distinctly set forth in her poems, writes Julian, which he described as mildly Calvinistic but without the severe dogmatic tenet of reprobation. He notes that the burden of her writings is a free and full salvation through the Redeemer's merits. Her life was devoted to the proclamation of this truth by personal labors, literary efforts, and earnest interest in Foreign Missions.

Julian notes that her hymns were frequently printed by J. & R. Parlane and by Caswell as leaflets.

Many of her hymns were published in Charles B. Snepp's *Songs of Grace and Glory* (London: James Nisbet, 1872, 1876, 1874, 1880, 1888), as well as several other noted hymn book collections in Great Britain and the United States. Her *Poetical Works*, edited by her sister Maria, was published in 1884 in two volumes by James Nisbet, London (855 pages; a PDF is available from the Internet Archive; http://www.archive.org/download/poeticalworksof-f00haveuoft/poeticalworksoff00haveuoft.pdf).

Please note that Ms. Havergal occasionally wrote verse in very lengthy lines. Short of resetting this book in smaller font size, it has been necessary to split lines, adjust tabs, and take other typographical measures to improve appearance without altering the meaning or meter.

Sources:

- John Julian, *Dictionary of Hymnology* (1892, Second Ed., 1907; republished by Dover Editions in 1957 in two volumes).

- David Chalkley, The Havergal Trust;
  http://www.havergaltrust.com/index.html ;
  Biographical note: http://www.havergaltrust.-
  com/frhavergal.html (site accessed May 26,
  2007).

Mizpah. Messages For Absent Friends

Source: Maria V. G. Havergal, ed., *The Poetical Works of Frances Ridley Havergal.* Toronto: Toronto Williard Tract Depot, ND (circa 1880), 405.

U PON the same bright morning star
Our gaze may meet, though severed far :
The Star of Bethlehem to-day
Shines brightly on our wintry way ;
And, gazing on its radiance clear ,
Our hearts may meet, and we are near !

Advent Thoughts

1877 at Newport

Source: Maria V. G. Havergal, ed., _The Poetical Works of Frances Ridley Havergal_. Toronto: Toronto Williard Tract Depot, ND (circa 1880), p. 743.

1

' Behold, the Bridegroom cometh ! ' MATT. xxv. 6.

O HERALD whisper falling
    Upon the passing night,
Mysteriously calling
    The Children of the Light !

He cometh ; oh, He cometh !
    Our own beloved Lord !
This blessed hope up-summeth
    Our undeserved reward.

He cometh ! Though the hour,
    Nor earth nor heaven may know,
Sure is the word of power,
    ' He cometh ! ' Even so !

2

Look up, and lift up your heads ; for your redemption
     draweth nigh.' - LUKE xxi. 28.

ADVENT shadows gather deep,
     Wars and desolations,
Troubled wakings, troubled sleep,
     Rushing of the nations.
Advent glory, grand and clear,
     Herald flashes flingeth ;
And the Judge who draweth near,
     Full salvation bringeth.

The Angels' Song

Source: Maria V. G. Havergal, ed., _The Poetical Works of Frances Ridley Havergal_. Toronto: Toronto Williard Tract Depot, ND (circa 1880), pp. 283-284.

N ow let us sing the Angels' Song,
    That rang so sweet and clear,
When heavenly light and music fell
    On earthly eye and ear, —
To Him we sing, our Saviour King,
    Who always deigns to hear:
        'Glory to God! and peace on earth.'

He came to tell the Father's love,
    His goodness, truth, and grace;
To show the brightness of His smile,
    The glory of His face;
With His own light, so full and bright,
    The shades of death to chase.
        'Glory to God ! and peace on earth.'

He came to bring the weary ones
    True peace and perfect rest ;
To take away the guilt and sin
    Which darkened and distressed;
That great and small might hear His call,
    And all in Him be blessed.
        'Glory to God ! and peace on earth.'

He came to bring a glorious gift,
  'Goodwill to men;' and why ?
Because He loved us, Jesus came
  For us to live and die.
Then, sweet and long, the Angels' Song
  Again we raise on high :
    'Glory to God ! and peace on earth.'

Sheet Music by A. Randegger from Charles L. Hutchins, _Carols Old and Carols New_. Boston: Parish Choir, 1916, #461, is available from my website, _The Hymns and Carols of Christmas_, www.hymnsandcarolsofchristmas.com

Leaving Us An Example, That Ye Should Follow His Steps

Source: Maria V. G. Havergal, ed., *The Poetical Works of Frances Ridley Havergal.* Toronto: Toronto Williard Tract Depot, ND (circa 1880), pp. 163-164.

O Jesu, Thou didst leave Thy glorious home,
  Of brightness more than mortal eye could bear,
And joys ineffable, alone to roam
Through earth's dark wilderness
in grief and want and care.
    Thou didst exchange the praise of seraph voices
      For sin-made discords and the wail of pain,
    The anthems swelling high
    where each in Thee rejoices
For fierce revilings in the world
where unbelief doth reign.
    Yes, Thou didst leave Thy bliss-encircled dwelling,
      Of joy and holiness and perfect love,
    And earnest to this world of sorrow, telling
      Each weary one the way to realms of rest above.
    Mark we Thy walk along the holy way,
      Each step is graven, that all the path may trace
    Which leads where Thou art gone, and never may
      The powers of darkness one bright step erase !
    And Thou hast left a solemn word behind Thee,
      Solemn, yet fraught with blessing ;
      would we learn
    How we may gain Thy dwelling,
    and there find Thee ?

Thou sayest, ' Follow Me.'
Be this our great concern.
And oh how blessed thus to mark each hour
The footsteps of our Saviour, and to know
That in them we are treading, then each flower
Of hope seems fairer,
and each joy doth yet more brightly glow.
Oh that I always followed Him alone !
I know that I am His, for I have bowed
In peaceful faith before my Saviour's throne,
And gladly there to Him
my life, my all, have vowed.
And He hath pardoned me, and washed away
Each stain of guilt,
and bade me quickly rise
And follow Him each moment of each day ;
And He hath set a crown
of life and joy before mine eyes.
How can I turn aside and wound the love
That gave Himself to bleed and die for me !
How can I stray, and grieve the holy Dove
Who lights my soul, opening mine eyes to see !
O Saviour, fix my wayward, wandering heart
Upon Thyself, that I may closely cling
To Thy blest side, and never more depart
From Thee, my loved Redeemer,
Thee, my heart's own King.
And grant me daily grace to follow Thee
Through joy and pleasure,
or through grief and sadness,
Until an entrance is vouchsafed to me
In Thy bright home of holiness and gladness.

No, Not A Star

(ANSWER TO A REMARK.)

1859 at Worcestershire

Source: Maria V. G. Havergal, ed., *The Poetical Works of Frances Ridley Havergal*. Toronto: Toronto Williard Tract Depot, ND (circa 1880), pp. 188-189.

N o, not a *star* !
    that is a name too beautiful and bright
For any earthly lay to wear,
    in this our lingering night ;
But 'mid the broken waters
    of our ever-restless thought,
My verse should be an answering gleam
    from highest radiance caught ;
That when through dark o'erarching boughs
    of sorrow, doubt, and sin,
The glorious Star of Bethlehem
    upon the flood looks in,
Its tiny trembling ray may bid
    some downcast vision turn
To that enkindling Light,
    for which all earthly shadows yearn.

No, not a _rainbow_ !
　　though upon the tearful cloud it trace
Sweet messages of sparing love,
　　of changeless truth and grace.
The daughter of its meekest hue
　　I would my verse might prove,
The leaf-veiled violet, that wins
　　so many a childish love ;
For little hearts no wounding thorn
　　or poison-cup to bear,
But pleasant fragrance and delight
　　to greet them everywhere.
I grieve not though each blossom
　　fall with swiftly ripening spring,
If o'er one eager face a smile of gladness
　　it may fling.

No, not a _fountain_ !
　　though it seem to spread white angelwings,
And soar aloft in spirit guise,
　　no gentle help it brings ;
It lives for its own loveliness alone,
　　then seeks once more
The chilly bosom of the rock
　　it slumbered in before.
Oh, be my verse a hidden stream
　　which silently may flow
Where drooping leaf and thirsty flower
　　in lonely valleys grow;
Till, blending with the broad bright stream
　　of sanctified endeavour,
God's glory be its ocean home,
　　the end it seeketh ever !

Advent Song

Nov. 16, 1873 at Winterdyne

Source: Maria V. G. Havergal, ed., *The Poetical Works of Frances Ridley Havergal*. Toronto: Toronto Williard Tract Depot, ND (circa 1880), pp. 497-499.

Thou art coming, O my Saviour !
    Thou art coming, O my King !
In Thy beauty all-resplendent,
In Thy glory all-transcendent ;
    Well may we rejoice and sing !
Coming ! in the opening east,
    Herald brightness slowly swells ;
Coming ! O my glorious Priest,
    Hear we not Thy golden bells ?

Thou art coming, Thou art coming !
    We shall meet Thee on Thy way,
We shall see Thee, we shall know Thee,
We shall bless Thee, we shall show Thee
    All our hearts could never say !
What an anthem that will be,
Ringing out our love to Thee,
Pouring out our rapture sweet
At Thine own all-glorious feet !

Thou art coming ! Rays of glory,
　　Through the veil Thy death has rent,
Touch the mountain and the river
With a golden glowing quiver,
　　Thrill of light and music blent.
Earth is brightened when this gleam
Falls on flower and rock and stream ;
Life is brightened when this ray
Falls upon its darkest day.

Not a cloud and not a shadow,
　　Not a mist and not a tear,
Not a sin and not a sorrow,
Not a dim and veiled to-morrow,
　　For that sunrise grand and clear !
Jesus, Saviour, once with Thee,
　　Nothing else seems worth a thought !
Oh, how marvellous will be
　　All the bliss Thy pain hath bought !

Thou art coming ! At Thy table
　　We are witnesses for this,
While remembering hearts Thou meetest,
In communion clearest, sweetest,
　　Earnest of our coming bliss.
Showing not Thy death alone,
　　And Thy love exceeding great,
But Thy coming and Thy throne,
　　All for which we long and wait.

Victorian Visions

Thou art coming ! We are waiting
    With a hope that cannot fail ;
Asking not the day or hour,
Resting on Thy word of power
    Anchored safe within the veil.
Time appointed may be long,
    But the vision must be sure :
Certainty shall make us strong,
    Joyful patience can endure !

Oh, the joy to see Thee reigning,
    Thee, my own beloved Lord !
Every tongue Thy name confessing,
Worship, honour, glory, blessing,
    Brought to Thee with glad accord !
Thee, my Master and my Friend,
    Vindicated and enthroned !
Unto earth's remotest end
    Glorified, adored, and owned !

Sheet Music, "Beverly," by William H. Monk, 1875,
from *The Parish School Hymnal.* Philadelphia: Board
of Publication of the United Lutheran Church in
America, 1926, #11, is available from my website, *The
Hymns and Carols of Christmas,*
www.hymnsandcarolsofchristmas.com

The Titles of Christ

1877 at Winterdyne

Source: Maria V. G. Havergal, ed., *The Poetical Works of Frances Ridley Havergal*. Toronto: Toronto Williard Tract Depot, ND (circa 1880), pp. 379-381.

Wonderful.

'For unto us a child is born, unto us a son is given ; and the government shall be upon His shoulder : and His Name shall be called Wonderful, Counsellor, The Mighty God, The Everlasting Father, The Prince of Peace.' ISA. ix. 6.

WONDERFUL ! Wonderful !
Ring out the Name, O Christmas chimes !
Wonderful ! Wonderful !
Echo the word to farthest climes !
May the splendour of this great Name
Shine and glow with a mighty flame,
Filling thy life with its glorious rays,
Filling thy spirit with Christmas praise.

Counsellor.

MIST and cloud and darkness
    Veil the wintry hour,
But the sun dispels them
    With his rising power.

Mist and cloud and darkness
    Often dim thy day,
But a Christmas glory
    Shines upon thy way.

May the Lord of Christmas,
    Counsellor and Friend,
Light thy desert pathway
    Even to the end.

Everlasting Father.

O NAME of gentlest grace,
O Name of strength and might,
Meeting the heart-need of our orphaned race
    With tenderest delight !
Our Everlasting Father ! This is He
    Who came in deep humility
    A little child to be !

The Mighty God.

THE Christmas bells proclaim
   His glorious name,
   'The Mighty God!'
God manifest indeed,

And yet the Woman's Seed,
   To whom we sing
   All glory, praise, and laud !
Divinest Lord and King.

The Prince Of Peace.

O NAME of beauty and of calm !
   O Name of rest and balm,
   Of exquisite delight,
And yet of sovereignty and might !
Let it make music in thy heart to-day,
And bid thee go rejoicing on thy way ;
For Jesus is thy Peace, thy Prince of Peace,
Whose reign within thy heart shall evermore increase.

Man Of Rest.

' Behold, a son shall be born to thee, who shall be a
man of rest,' I CHRON. xxii. 9.

HAIL, Christmas morn !
For unto us the Son is born,
    The Man of Rest !
    The weary quest
Is over now, for He who cometh, calleth,
' Come unto Me, and I will give you rest ! '
    The still voice falleth
On hearts that, listening, are blessed.
    And daily shall the blessing flow,
    And daily shall the gladness grow,
For we which have believed do enter into rest.

Note: This series of verses are similar in theme to the
"Great Antiphons" from antiquity that formed the
basis for the John Mason Neale hymn "O Come, O
Come, Emmanuel"
http://www.hymnsandcarolsofchristmas.com/Hymns
_and_Carols/o_come_o_come_emmanuel-1.htm

And see:
- "The Great Advent Antiphons."
  http://www.hymnsandcarolsofchristmas.com/
  Hymns_and_Carols/Notes_On_Carols/O_Antip
  hons/great_advent_antiphons.htm

- "The O Antiphons"
  http://www.hymnsandcarolsofchristmas.com/
  Hymns and Carols/Notes On Carols/O Antip
  hons/o antiphons.htm
- "The Prose Antiphons"
  http://www.hymnsandcarolsofchristmas.com/
  Hymns and Carols/Notes On Carols/O Antip
  hons/prose antiphons.htm

Bells Across The Snow

1870 at Oakhampton

Source: Maria V. G. Havergal, ed., *The Poetical Works
of Frances Ridley Havergal.* Toronto: Toronto Williard
Tract Depot, ND (circa 1880), pp. 619-620.

O CHRISTMAS, merry Christmas !
    Is it really come again ?
With its memories and greetings,
    With its joy and with its pain.
There's a minor in the carol,
    And a shadow in the light,
And a spray of cypress twining
    With the holly wreath to-night.
And the hush is never broken
    By laughter light and low,
As we listen in the starlight
    To the 'bells across the snow.'

O Christmas, merry Christmas !
    'T is not so very long
Since other voices blended
    With the carol and the song !
If we could but hear them singing
    As they are singing now,

If we could but see the radiance
    Of the crown on each dear brow ;
There would be no sigh to smother,
    No hidden tear to flow,
As we listen in the starlight
    To the ' bells across the snow.'

O Christmas, merry Christmas !
    This never more can be ;
We cannot bring again the days
    Of our unshadowed glee.
But Christmas, happy Christmas,
    Sweet herald of goodwill,
With holy songs of glory
    Brings holy gladness still.
For peace and hope may brighten,
    And patient love may glow,
As we listen in the starlight
    To the ' bells across the snow.'

Also found in *Christmas: Its Origin, Celebration and Significance as Related in Prose and Verse* - Robert Haven Schauffler, 1907.

Sheet Music by Myles B. Foster, from Rev. Charles Lewis Hutchins, *Carols Old and Carols New*. Boston: Parish Choir, 1916, Carol 334, is available at my website, *The Hymns and Carols of Christmas*, www.hymnsandcarolsofchristmas.com

The Happiest Christmas Day

Source: Maria V. G. Havergal, ed., *The Poetical Works of Frances Ridley Havergal.* Toronto: Toronto Williard Tract Depot, ND (circa 1880), p. 303-304.

SYBIL, my little one, come away,
I have a plan for Christmas Day :
Put on your hat, and trot with me,
A dear little suffering girl to see.

Tis not very far, and there's plenty of time,
For the bells have not begun to chime ;
So, Sybil, over the sparkling snow
To dear little Lizzie let us go.

Dear little Lizzie is ill and weak,
Only just able to smile and speak.
Yesterday morning I stood by her bed ;
Now, shall I tell you what she said ?

' Christmas is coming to-morrow,' said I.
' I shall be happy ! ' was Lizzie's reply ;
' Happy, *so* happy ! ' I wish you had heard
How sweetly and joyously rang that word.

' Dear little Lizzie, lying in pain,
With never a hope to be better again,
Lying so lonely, what will you do ?
Why will the day be so happy to you ? '

Lizzie looked up with a smile as bright
As if she were full of some new delight ;
And the sweet little lips just parted to say,
' I shall think of Jesus all Christmas Day !'

How would you like to take her the spray
Of red-berried holly I gave you to-day ?
And what if we gave her the pretty wreath too
That Bertha has made with ivy and yew?

The green and the scarlet would brighten the gloom
Of dear little Lizzie's shady room ;
And, Sybil, I know she would like us to sing
A Christmas song of the new-born King.

Sybil, my little one, if we do,
It will help us to ' think of Jesus ' too ;
And Lizzie was right, for that is the way
To have the happiest Christmas Day !

The Disappointed Carol Singers

Alternate Title:
Oh, Must We Not Sing Our Christmas Hymn

Source: Maria V. G. Havergal, ed., *The Poetical Works of Frances Ridley Havergal.* Toronto: Toronto Williard Tract Depot, ND (circa 1880), p. 302.

OH, must we not sing our Christmas hymn,
  And will you not hear our song ?
With joyous voice, but with weary limb,
  We have roamed the whole day long !

We have thought of the merry Christmas time
  For many a week before,
And have gleefully learnt our Christmas rhyme
  To carol at your door.

There are no merry larks to wake you now,
  No blackbirds in woody dell ;
The nightingale loves not the leafless bough,
  The humming bee sleeps in his cell.

Oh, winter is gloomy and dark enough,
  And must it be silent too ?
Are the chorus of winds and the storm-song rough
  The only sweet music for you ?

But we are the birds of the winter day,
    When all else is dark and still ;
Then, lady, send us not all away,
    And with sorrow our eager hearts fill.

Oh, do not thus wave your beautiful hand,
    And bid us unheard to go;
For the carolling time of our little band
    Comes but once a year, you know.

Amid The Broken Waters

Prelude to _Ministry Of Song_

Source: Maria V. G. Havergal, ed., _The Poetical Works
of Frances Ridley Havergal._ Toronto: Toronto Williard
Tract Depot, ND (circa 1880), p. 9.

A MID the broken waters
of our ever-restless thought,
Oh be my verse an answering gleam
from higher radiance caught ;
That where through dark o'er arching boughs
of sorrow, doubt, and sin,
The glorious Star of Bethlehem
upon the flood looks in,
Its tiny trembling ray may bid
some downcast vision turn
To that enkindling Light,
for which all earthly shadows yearn.
Oh be my verse a hidden stream,
which silently may flow
Where drooping leaf and thirsty flower
in lonely valleys grow;
And often by its shady course
to pilgrim hearts be brought
The quiet and refreshment
of an upward-pointing thought ;
Till, blending with the broad bright stream
of sanctified endeavour,
God's glory be its ocean home,
the end it seeketh ever.

An Indian Flag

Source: Maria V. G. Havergal, ed., *The Poetical Works of Frances Ridley Havergal.* Toronto: Toronto Williard Tract Depot, ND (circa 1880), pp. 528-530.

THE golden gates were opening
    For another welcome guest ;
For a ransomed heir of glory
    Was entering into rest :

The first in far Umritsur
    Who heard the joyful sound,
The first who came to Jesus
    Within its gloomy bound.

The wonderers and the watchers
    Around his dying bed,
Saw Christ's own fearless witness
    Safe through the valley led.

And they whose faithful sowing
    Had not been all in vain,
Knew that the angels waited
    Their sheaf of ripened grain.

He spoke : ' Throughout the city
    How many a flag is raised
Where loveless deities are owned,
    And powerless gods are praised !

Victorian Visions

' I give my house to Jesus,
  That it may always be
A flag for Christ, the Son of God,
  Who gave Himself for me. '

And now in far Umritsur
  That flag is waving bright,
Amid the heathen darkness,
  A clear and shining light.

A house where all may gather
  The words of peace to hear,
And seek the only Saviour
  Without restraint or fear ;

Where patient toil of teaching,
  And kindly deeds abound ;
Where holy festivals are kept,
  And holy songs resound.

First convert of Umritsur,
  Well hast thou led the way ;
Now, who will rise and follow ?
  Who dares to answer, ' Nay ' ?

O children of salvation !
  O dwellers in the light !
Have ye no ' flag for Jesus, '
  Far-waving, fair, and bright ?

Will ye not band together,
    And, working hand in hand,
Set up a ' flag for Jesus, '
    In that wide heathen land ?

In many an Indian city,
    Oh, let a standard wave,
Our gift of love and honour,
    To Him who came to save ;

To Him beneath whose banner
    Of wondrous love we rest ;
Our Friend, the Friend of sinners,
    The Greatest and the Best.

A Merry Christmas

Source: J. F. Kinsey and John McPherson, eds.,
Echoes Of Glory For The Sunday School. LaFayette,
Indiana: The Echo Music Company, 1888.

A Merry Christmas to you!
　　For we that serve the Lord with mirth,
And we carol forth glad tidings
　　Of our holy Saviour's birth.
So we keep the olden greeting
　　With its meaning deep and true,
And wish a Merrie Christmas
　　And a Happy New Year to you!

Oh, yes! a Merrie Christmas
　　With blithest song and smile,
Bright with the thought of him who dwelt
　　On earth a little while,
That we might dwell forever
　　Where never falls a tear;
So a Merrie Christmas to you,
　　And a happy, happy year.

Christmas Mottoes

1877 at Winterdyne

Source: Maria V. G. Havergal, ed., *The Poetical Works of Frances Ridley Havergal.* Toronto: Toronto Williard Tract Depot, ND (circa 1880), pp. 372-374.

1

UNTO you the Child is born,
On this blessed Christmas morn.
Unto you, to be your Peace ;
    Unto you, for He hath found you ;
Unto you, with full release
    From the weary chains that bound you:
Unto you, that you may rise
Unto Him above the skies.

2

THE wilderness shall rejoice,
    And the wintry waste shall sing,
At the wakening herald voice
    Of the coming of the King.
So the sparkling Christmas snow
    Is dearer than summer light ;
For He whom we love came down below
    In the hush of a Christmas night.
May thy Christmas morning break
    Holy and bright and calm ;

And may all thy life for His dear sake
    Be a joyful Christmas psalm.

3

    Is it a wintry night ?
    Watch ! for the heavenly light
Shineth, O mourner, around and above !
    Tidings of joy to thee
    Float on the minstrelsy !
Rise up and welcome the Son of His love.

4

    Behold, thy King cometh unto thee.' ZECH. ix. 9.

    COMETH in lowliness,
    Cometh in righteousness,
Cometh in mercy all royal and free !
    Cometh with grace and might,
    Cometh with love and light ;
Cometh, beloved ! He cometh to thee !

5

    BRIGHT be thy Christmas tide !
    Carol it far and wide,
Jesus, the King and the Saviour, is come !
    Jesus thy guest will be ;
    O let Him dwell with thee !
Open thy heart for His palace and home.

WHAT do the angels sing?
What is the word they bring ?
What is the music of Christmas again ?
Glad tidings still to thee,
Peace and good-will to thee,
Glory to God in the highest ! Amen.

6

OH, Christmas blessings cannot cease,
Christmas joy is deep and strong !
For Christ is come to be our Peace,
Our Salvation and our Song.

Christmas Gifts

Source: Maria V. G. Havergal, ed., *The Poetical Works of Frances Ridley Havergal.* Toronto: Toronto Williard Tract Depot, ND (circa 1880), pp. 374-375.

1

THE wondrous love and light,
    The fulness and the glory,
The meaning and the might
    Of all the Christmas story,
May Christ Himself unfold to you to-day,
And bid you go rejoicing on your way.

2

A HAPPY, happy Christmas
    Be yours to-day !
Oh, not the failing measure
Of fleeting earthly pleasure,
But Christmas joy abiding,
While years are swiftly gliding,
    Be yours, I pray,
Through Him who gave us Christmas Day !

3

A BRIGHT and blessed Christmas Day,
    With echoes of the angels' song,
And peace that cannot pass away,
    And holy gladness, calm and strong,
And sweet heart carols, flowing free !
This is my Christmas wish to thee !

4

DOWN the ages hoary
Peals the song of glory,
Peace, and God's good-will !
Other echoes die away,
But the song of Christmas Day
Echoes from the Judean hill,
Ever clearer, louder still.
Oh, may its holy, heavenly chime
Make all thy life a Christmas time !

A Happy Christmas

May 1877 at Winterdyne

Source: Maria V. G. Havergal, ed., *The Poetical Works of Frances Ridley Havergal.* Toronto: Toronto Williard Tract Depot, ND (circa 1880), pp. 369-370.

A HAPPY Christmas to you !
 For the Light of Life is born,
And His coming is the sunshine
 Of the dark and wintry morn.
The grandest orient glow must pale,
The loveliest western gleams must fail :
 But His great Light,
 So full, so bright,
Ariseth for thy heart to-day ;
His shadow-conquering beams shall never pass away.

A happy Christmas to you !
 For the Prince of Peace is come,
And His reign is full of blessings,
 Their very crown and sum.
No earthly calm can ever last,
'Tis but the lull before the blast:
 But His great peace
 Shall still increase
In mighty, all-rejoicing sway;
His kingdom in thy heart shall never pass away.

Frances Ridley Havergal

Christmas Sunshine

Dec. 25, 1887 at Winterdyne

Source: Maria V. G. Havergal, ed., *The Poetical Works of Frances Ridley Havergal.* Toronto: Toronto Williard Tract Depot, ND (circa 1880), pp. 375-379.

1

Do the angels know the blessed day,
    And strike their harps anew ?
Then may the echo of their lay
    Float sweetly down to you,
And fill your soul with Christmas song
That your heart shall echo your whole life long.

2

JESUS came ! and came for me !
    Simple words ! and yet expressing
Depths of holy mystery,
    Depths of wondrous love and blessing.

3

Holy Spirit, make me see
All His coming means for me ;
Take the things of Christ, I pray,
Show them to my heart to-day.

4

OH, let thy heart make melody,
    And thankful songs uplift,
For Christ Himself is come to be
    Thy glorious Christmas gift.

5

A HAPPY, happy Christmas,
    And a happy, happy year !
Oh, we have not deserved it,
    And yet we need not fear.
For Jesus has deserved it,
    And so, for Jesus' sake,
This cup of joy and blessing
    With grateful hand we take.

5

THERE is silence high in the midnight sky,
    And only the sufferers watch the night ;
But long ago there was song and glow,
    And a message of joy from the Prince of Light,
And the Christmas song of the messenger-throng
The echoes of life shall for ever prolong.

7

GREAT is the mystery
    Of wondrous grace,
God manifest we see
    In Jesu's face.

O deepest mystery
    Of Love Divine,
God manifest for me,
    And Jesus mine !

8

WHAT was the first angelic word
That the startled shepherds heard ?
' Fear not ! ' Beloved, it comes to you
As a Christmas message most sweet and true,
As true for you as it was for them
In the lonely fields of Bethlehem ;
And as sweet to-day as it was that night,
When the glory dazzled their mortal sight.

9

CHRIST is come to be my Friend,
    Leading, loving to the end ;
Christ is come to be my King,
    Ordering, ruling everything.
Christ is come ! Enough for me,
Lonely though the pathway be.

10

GIVE me a song, O Lord,
    That I may sing to Thee,
In true and sweet accord
    With angel minstrelsy.
Oh, tune my heart that it may bring
A Christmas anthem to my King.

11

SWELL the notes of the Christmas Song !
    Sound it forth through the earth abroad !
    Glory to God !
    Blessing and honour, thanks and laud !
Take the joy of the Christmas Song !
    Are not the tidings good and true ?
    Peace to you,
    And God's good-will that is ever new !

12

CHRIST is come to be thy light,
Shining through the darkest night ;
He will make thy pilgrim way
Shine unto the perfect day.
Take the message ! let it be
Full of Christmas joy to thee !

A Merrie Christmas

Oct. 1875 at Whitby

Source: Maria V. G. Havergal, ed., *The Poetical Works of Frances Ridley Havergal*. Toronto: Toronto Williard Tract Depot, ND (circa 1880), p. 369.

A MERRIE *Christmas* to you !
   For we serve the Lord with mirth,
And we carol forth glad tidings
   Of our holy Saviour's birth.
So we keep the olden greeting
   With its meaning deep and true,
And wish ' a merrie Christmas '
   And a happy New Year to you I

Oh, yes ! ' a merrie Christmas, '
   With blithest song and smile,
Bright with the thought of Him who dwelt
   On earth a little while,
That we might dwell for ever
   Where never falls a tear :
So ' a merrie Christmas ' to you,
   And a happy, happy year !

New Year Hymn

Source: Maria V. G. Havergal, ed., *The Poetical Works of Frances Ridley Havergal.* Toronto: Toronto Williard Tract Depot, ND (circa 1880), pp. 350-352.

J ESUS, blessed Saviour,
    Help us now to raise
Songs of glad thanksgiving,
    Songs of holy praise.
O how kind and gracious
    Thou hast always been !
O how many blessings
    Every day has seen !
        Jesus, blessed Saviour,
            Now our praises hear,
        For Thy grace and favour
            Crowning all the year.

Jesus, holy Saviour,
    Only Thou canst tell
How we often stumbled,
    How we often fell !
All our sins (so many !),
    Saviour, Thou dost know ;
In Thy blood most precious,
    Wash us white as snow.
        Jesus, blessed Saviour,
            Keep us in Thy fear,
        Let Thy grace and favour
            Pardon all the year.

Frances Ridley Havergal

Jesus, loving Saviour,
    Only Thou dost know
All that may befall us
    As we onward go.
So we humbly pray Thee,
    Take us by the hand,
Lead us ever upward
    To the Better Land.
        Jesus, blessed Saviour,
            Keep us ever near,
        Let Thy grace and favour
            Shield us all the year.

Jesus, precious Saviour,
    Make us all Thine own,
Make us Thine for ever,
    Make us Thine alone.
Let each day, each moment,
    Of this glad New-year,
Be for Jesus only,
    Jesus, Saviour dear.
        Then, O blessed Saviour,
            Never need we fear,
        For Thy grace and favour
            Crown our bright New-year !

Christmas Gifts

May 1877 at Winterdyne

Source: Maria V. G. Havergal, ed., *The Poetical Works of Frances Ridley Havergal.* Toronto: Toronto Williard Tract Depot, ND (circa 1880), pp. 371-372.

' Thou hast received gifts for men. ' Ps. lxviii. 18.

C HRISTMAS gifts for thee,
    Fair and free !
Precious things from the heavenly store,
Filling thy casket more and more ;
Golden love in divinest chain,
That never can be untwined again ;
Silvery carols of joy that swell
Sweetest of all in the heart's lone cell ;
Pearls of peace that were sought for thee
In the terrible depths of a fiery sea ;
Diamond promises sparkling bright,
Flashing in farthest reaching light

      Christmas gifts for thee,
      Grand and free !

Christmas gifts from the King of love,
Brought from His royal home above ;
Brought to thee in the far-off land,
Brought to thee by His own dear hand.
Promises held by Christ for thee,
Peace as a river flowing free,
Joy that in His own joy must live,
And love that Infinite Love can give.
Surely thy heart of hearts uplifts
Carols of praise for such Christmas gifts !

Our Saviour Christ Was Born

May 1877 at Winterdyne

Source: Maria V. G. Havergal, ed., _The Poetical Works of Frances Ridley Havergal_. Toronto: Toronto Williard Tract Depot, ND (circa 1880), pp. 370-371.

OUR Saviour Christ was born
That we might have the rose without the thorn ;
    All through His desert life
He felt the thorns of human sin and strife.
    His blessed feet were bare
To every hurting brier ; He did not spare
One bleeding footstep on the way
He came to trace for us, until the day
The cruel crown was pressed upon the Brow,
That smiles upon us from His glory now.

    And so He won for us
Sweet, thornless, everlasting flowers thus ;
    He bids our desert way
Rejoice and blossom as the rose to-day.
    There is no hidden thorn
In His good gifts of grace ; He would adorn
The lives that now are His alone,
With brightness and with beauty all His own.
Then praise the Lord who came on Christmas Day
To give the rose and take the thorns away.

New Year Verses
Pages 385 - 396

A Happy New Year To You

1874 at Winterdyne

Source: Maria V. G. Havergal, ed., *The Poetical Works of Frances Ridley Havergal*. Toronto: Toronto Williard Tract Depot, ND (circa 1880), p. 385.

NEW mercies, new blessings,
    new light on thy way ;
New courage, new hope,
    and new strength for each day ;
New notes of thanksgiving, new chords of delight,
New praise in the morning, new songs in the night ;
New wine in thy chalice, new altars to raise ;
New fruits for thy Master, new garments of praise ;
New gifts from His treasures,
    new smiles from His face ;
New streams from the fountain of infinite grace ;
New stars for thy crown, and new tokens of love ;
New gleams of the glory that waits thee above ;
New light of His countenance full and unpriced ;
All this be the joy of thy new life in Christ !

Faithful Promises

ISA. xli. 10.

New Year's Hymn

Jan. 3, 1873 at Winterdyne

Source: Maria V. G. Havergal, ed., *The Poetical Works of Frances Ridley Havergal.* Toronto: Toronto Williard Tract Depot, ND (circa 1880), pp. 386-388.

STANDING at the portal
    Of the opening year,
Words of comfort meet us,
    Hushing every fear ;
Spoken through the silence
    By our Father's voice,
Tender, strong, and faithful,
    Making us rejoice.
Onward then, and fear not,
    Children of the day !
For His word shall never,
    Never pass away!

I, the Lord am with thee,
    Be thou not afraid !
I will help and strengthen,
    Be thou not dismayed !
Yea, I will uphold thee
    With my own right hand ;
Thou art called and chosen
    In my sight to stand.
Onward then, and fear not,
    Children of the day !
For His word shall never,
    Never pass away !

For the year before us,
    Oh, what rich supplies !
For the poor and needy
    Living streams shall rise ;
For the sad and sinful
    Shall His grace abound ;
For the faint and feeble
    Perfect strength be found.
Onward then, and fear not,
    Children of the day !
For His word shall never,
    Never pass away !

Victorian Visions

He will never fail us,
     He will not forsake ;
His eternal covenant
     He will never break !
Resting on His promise,
     What have we to fear?
God is all-sufficient
     For the coming year.
Onward then, and fear not.
     Children of the day !
For His word shall never,
     Never pass away !

A Happy New Year

1874 at Winterdyne

Source: Maria V. G. Havergal, ed., *The Poetical Works of Frances Ridley Havergal.* Toronto: Toronto Williard Tract Depot, ND (circa 1880), pp. 389-390.

A HAPPY New Year ! Oh such may it be !
Joyously, surely, and fully for thee !
Fear not and faint not, but be of good cheer,
And trustfully enter thy happy New Year !

Happy, so happy ! Thy Father shall guide,
Protect thee, preserve thee, and always provide !
Onward and upward along the right way
Lovingly leading thee day by day.

Happy, so happy ! Thy Saviour shall be
Ever more precious and present with thee !
Happy, so happy ! His Spirit thy Guest,
Filling with glory the place of His rest.

Happy, so happy ! Though shadows around
May gather and darken, they flee at the sound
Of the glorious Voice that saith, ' Be of good cheer !'
Then joyously enter thy happy New Year !

New Year's Wishes

Sept. 1874 at Ormont Dessous

Source: Maria V. G. Havergal, ed., *The Poetical Works of Frances Ridley Havergal.* Toronto: Toronto Williard Tract Depot, ND (circa 1880), pp. 388-389.

W HAT shall I wish thee ?
        Treasures of earth ?
Songs in the spring-time,
        Pleasure and mirth ?
Flowers on thy pathway,
        Skies ever clear ?
Would this ensure thee
        A Happy New Year ?

What shall I wish thee ?
        What can be found
Bringing thee sunshine
        All the year round ?
Where is the treasure,
        Lasting and dear,
That shall ensure thee
        A Happy New Year ?

Faith that increaseth,
    Walking in light ;
Hope that aboundeth,
    Happy and bright ;
Love that is perfect,
    Casting out fear ;
These shall ensure thee
    A Happy New Year.

Peace in the Saviour,
    Rest at His feet,
Smile of His countenance
    Radiant and sweet,
Joy in His presence,
    Christ ever near !
This will ensure thee
    A Happy New Year !

Another Year

1874 at Winterdyne

Source: Maria V. G. Havergal, ed., *The Poetical Works of Frances Ridley Havergal.* Toronto: Toronto Williard Tract Depot, ND (circa 1880), p. 385-386.

A NOTHER year is dawning !
Dear Master, let it be,
In working or in waiting,
Another year with Thee.

Another year of leaning
Upon Thy loving breast,
Of ever-deepening trustfulness,
Of quiet, happy rest.

Another year of mercies,
Of faithfulness and grace ;
Another year of gladness
In the shining of Thy face.

Another year of progress,
Another year of praise ;
Another year of proving
Thy presence 'all the days.'

Another year of service,
  Of witness for Thy love ;
Another year of training
  For holier work above.

Another year is dawning,
  Dear Master, let it be,
On earth, or else in heaven,
  Another year for Thee !

New Year Mottoes

1876-1879 at Winterdyne

Source: Maria V. G. Havergal, ed., *The Poetical Works of Frances Ridley Havergal.* Toronto: Toronto Williard Tract Depot, ND (circa 1880), pp. 390-396.

1

'From this day will I bless you.' HAG. ii 19.

FROM this day
' He shall bless thee !
What shall then distress thee ?
   ' From this day '
He will never leave thee ;
What shall grieve thee ?
Christ, thy mighty Friend,
Loveth to the end
   ' From this day !'

2

'Be glad and rejoice, for the Lord will do great things.'
JOEL ii. 21.

THE Lord *hath* done great things for thee !
   All through the fleeted days
Jehovah hath dealt wondrously ;
   Lift up thy heart and praise !

For greater things thine eyes shall see,
  Child of His loving choice !
The Lord will do great things for thee ;
  Fear not, be glad, rejoice !

  Wondrously
The Lord *hath* dealt with thee !
  Wondrous mercy all the way,
  Wondrous patience every day,
  Wondrous pardon, wondrous feeling,
  Wondrous help and wondrous leading
  Through the bygone year.
  Wondrously
The Lord *shall* deal with thee !
  Wondrous tenderness and grace,
  Wondrous shining of His face,
  Wondrous faithfulness and power,
  Wondrous love, shall twine each bower
  Through the coming year !

3

Crown the year with Thy goodness, Lord !
  And make every hour a gem
  In the living diadem,
    That sparkles to Thy praise.

Crown the year with Thy grace, O Lord !
  Be Thy fresh anointings shed
  On Thy waiting servant's head,
    Who treads Thy royal ways.

CROWN the year with Thy glory, Lord !
　　Let the brightness and the glow
　　Of its heavenly overflow
　　　　Crown Thy beloved's days !

STRONG and loving is thy Friend !
Trust Him for the untried year !
He shall lead thee to the end,
Ever gracious, ever near.
As the everlasting hills
Thou shalt find His faithfulness ;
As the crystal mountain-rills.

4

' And on the east side toward the rising of the sun
shall they of the standard of the camp of Judah pitch
throughout their armies: and Nahshon the son of
Amminadab shall be captain of the children of
Judah.' — NUM. ii. 3.

TOWARD the rising of the sun
　　Now thy standard raise !
Let thy New Year's halt be one
　　In the Camp of Praise.
Then the wilderness shall be
Fruitful, fair, and glad for thee.

5

ANOTHER year of patient toil,
A few sheaves won from rocky soil,
　　May seem not much to thee ;
But all thy work is with the Lord,
And thine exceeding great reward
　　Thy God Himself shall be.

6

PRAISING together for all the way,
　　Now let us welcome our New Year's Day,
Rejoicing together in faith and love,
　　Hoping together for rest above.

ETERNITY with Jesus
　　Is long enough for rest ;
Thank God that we are spared to work
　　For Him whom we love best !

7

' The Lord bless thee, and keep thee : The Lord make
His face shine upon thee, and be gracious unto thee :
The Lord lift up His countenance upon thee, and give
thee peace.' — NUM. vi. 24-26.

THE threefold blessing Israel heard
    Three thousand years ago,
God grant it may on thee to-day
    In power and fulness flow ;
That Light and Peace in grand increase
    All through the year may glow.

8

LORD JESUS, keep our dear one
    All through the year ;
By day and night Thy presence bright
    Be ever near ;
And Thy sweet word be always heard
    To guide and cheer.

9

' I will sing of mercy and judgment.' - Ps. ci. i.

ONE year less
Of wisely-ordered loss,
Of sorrow and of weariness,
    Conflict and cross.

One year more
Of mercies ever new,
Of love in never-failing store,
    Faithful and true.

10

' He it is that doth go before thee ; He will be with
thee, He will not fail thee.' - DEUT. xxxi. 8.

THE Lord thy God !
He it is that goes before thee,
His the banner waving o'er thee,
    Bright and broad !
When the fiercest foes assail thee,
He it is that will not fail thee,
    The Lord thy God !

11

' The righteous, and the wise, and their works, are in
the hand of God. - ECCLES. ix. 1.

THE future ! who may lift the veil
And read its yet unwritten tale ?
But sorrow and joy alike we leave
      In the Hand that doeth all things well,
And calmly from that Hand receive
      All that each coming year may tell.
We would not ask of life or death,
It shall be as the Master saith.

12

Now Thy loving Spirit
      On our lives outpour ;
Make us know Thee better,
      Make us love Thee more.

Take us now, we pray Thee,
      Make us all Thine own ;
Keep us Thine for ever,
      Keep us Thine alone !

13

' Nᴏᴛ as the world giveth
      Give I to you !'
Saith the Redeemer,
      Faithful and True.
May He enrich thee,
      This New Year's Day,
With gifts from His treasure
      That pass not away.

14

Tʜɪs New Year Thou givest me,
      Lord, I consecrate to Thee,
      With all its nights and days :
Fill my hand with service blest,
Fill my heart with holy rest,
      And fill my life with praise.

15

A ʙʀɪɢʜᴛ New Year, and a sunny track
      Along an upward way,
And a song of praise on looking back,
      When the year has passed away,
And golden sheaves nor small nor few !
This is my New Year's wish for you !

16

ANOTHER year for Jesus !
How can I wish for you
A greater joy or blessing,
O fellow-worker true ?
Is the work difficult ?
Jesus directs thee.
Is the path dangerous ?
Jesus protects thee.
Fear not, and falter not,
Let the word cheer thee !
All through the coming year
He will be with thee !

17

HAPPY, because He loves thee !
Happy, because He lives !
Bright with that deepest gladness
Which only Jesus gives.
Happy, because He guides thee.
Because He cares for thee ;
Happy, ever so happy,
Thus may thy New Year be !

18

FOR the weariest day
    May Christ be thy stay !
For the darkest night
    May Christ be thy light !
For the weakest hour
    May Christ be thy power !
For each moment's fall
    May Christ be thy All !

For New Year's Day, 1874

Dec. 23, 1873 at Winterdyne

Source: Maria V. G. Havergal, ed., *The Poetical Works of Frances Ridley Havergal.* Toronto: Toronto Williard Tract Depot, ND (circa 1880), pp. 660-663.

'From glory to glory.' - 2 Cor. iii. 18.

FROM glory unto glory !
    Be this our joyous song
As on the King's own highway
    we bravely march along !
' From glory unto glory !'
    O word of stirring cheer,
As dawns the solemn brightness
    of another glad New Year.

Our own beloved Master
    'hath many things to say;'
Look forward to His teaching,
    unfolding day by day;
To whispers of His Spirit,
    while resting at His feet,
To glowing revelation,
    to insight clear and sweet,

' From glory unto glory !'
   Our faith hath seen the King,
We own His matchless beauty,
   as adoringly we sing :
But He hath more to show us !
   O thought of untold bliss!
We press on exultingly
   in certain hope to this :—

To marvellous outpourings
   of His ' treasures new and old,'
To largess of His bounty,
   paid in the King's own gold,
To glorious expansion
   of His mysteries of grace,
To radiant unveilings
   of the brightness of His face,

' From glory unto glory !'
   What great things He hath done,
What wonders He hath shown us,
   what triumphs He hath won !
We marvel at the records
   of the blessings of the year !
But sweeter than the Christmas bells
   rings out His promise clear—

Victorian Visions

That 'greater things,' far greater,
    our longing eyes shall see!
We can but wait and wonder
    what 'greater things' shall be!
But glorious fulfilments
    rejoicingly we claim,
While pleading in the power
    of the All-prevailing Name.

' From glory unto glory ! '
    What mighty blessings crown
The lives for which our Lord
    hath laid His own so freely down !
Omnipotence to keep us,
    Omniscience to guide,
Jehovah's Triune Presence
    within us to abide !

The fulness of His blessing
    encompasseth our way ;
The fulness of His promises
    crowns every brightening day;
The fulness of His glory
    is beaming from above,
While more and more we realize
    the fulness of His love.

' From glory unto glory ! '
    Without a shade of care,
Because the Lord who loves us
    will every burden bear;
Because we trust Him fully,
    and know that He will guide,
And know that He will keep us
    at His beloved side.

' From glory unto glory ! '
    Though tribulation fall,
It cannot touch our treasure,
    when Christ is all in all !
Whatever lies before us,
    there can be naught to fear,
For what are pain and sorrow
    when Jesus Christ is near ?

' From glory unto glory ! '
    O marvels of the word !
' With open face beholding
    the glory of the Lord,'
We, even we (O wondrous grace !)
    ' are changed into the same,'
The image of our Saviour,
    to glorify His Name.

Victorian Visions

Abiding in His presence,
        and walking in the light,
And seeking to ' do always
        what is pleasing in His sight,'
We look to Him to keep us
        ' all glorious within,'
Because ' the blood of Jesus Christ
        is cleansing from all sin.'

The things behind forgetting,
        we only gaze before,
' From glory unto glory,'
        that ' shineth more and more,'
Because our Lord hath said it,
        that such shall be our way
(O splendour of the promise !)
        ' unto the perfect day.'

' From glory unto glory ! '
        Our fellow-travellers still
Are gathering on the journey !
        the bright electric thrill
Of quick instinctive union,
        more frequent and more sweet,
Shall swiftly pass from heart to heart
        in true and tender beat.

And closer yet, and closer
the golden bonds shall be,
Enlinking all who love our Lord
in pure sincerity ;
And wider yet, and wider
shall the circling glory glow;
As more and more are taught of God
that mighty love to know.

O ye who seek the Saviour,
look up in faith and love,
Come up into the sunshine,
so bright and warm above !
No longer tread the valley,
but, clinging to His hand,
Ascend the shining summits
and view the glorious land.

Our harp-notes should be sweeter,
our trumpet-tones more clear,
Our anthems ring so grandly,
that all the world must hear !
Oh, royal be our music,
for who hath cause to sing
Like the chorus of redeemed ones,
the Children of the King!

Victorian Visions

Oh, let our adoration
    for all that He hath done
Peal out beyond the stars of God,
    while voice and life are one !
And let our consecration be real,
    and deep, and true ;
Oh, even now our hearts shall bow,
    and joyful vows renew !

' In full and glad surrender
    we give ourselves to Thee,
Thine utterly, and only,
    and evermore to be !
O Son of God, who lovest us,
    we will be Thine alone,
And all we are, and all we have,
    shall henceforth be Thine own !

' Now, onward, ever onward,
    from ' strength to strength ' we go.
While 'grace for grace' abundantly
    shall from His fulness flow,
To glory's full fruition,
    from glory's foretaste here,
Until His Very Presence crown
    our happiest New Year !

Note:
  This poem was frequently adapted (and altered) as a
hymn as early as 1889. A version from the venerable
Hymns Ancient and Modern is found below.

From Glory Unto Glory

For New Year's Day

Words: Frances Ridley Havergal (1836-1879)
Music: "St. Colomb," W. S. Hoyte
Meter: 76 76 76 86

Source: W. H. Monk and C. Steggall, eds., *Hymns Ancient and Modern*. London, William Clowes and Sons, Old Edition, 1889, Hymn 485, p. 573.

1. From glory unto glory!
     Be this our joyous song,
As on the King's own highway,
     we bravely march along!
From glory unto glory!
     O word of stirring cheer,
As dawns the solemn brightness
     of another glad New Year.

2. From glory unto glory!
     What great things He hath done,
What wonders He hath shown us,
     what triumphs He hath won!
What glory unto glory!
     What mighty blessings crown
The lives for which our Lord hath
     laid His own so freely down!

3. The fulness of His blessings
    encompasseth our way;
The fulness of His promises
    crowns every bright'ning day;
The fulness of His glory
    is beaming from above,
While more and more we learn
    to know the fulness of His love.

4. And closer yet and closer
    the golden bonds shall be,
Uniting all who love our Lord
    in pure sincerity;
And wider yet and wider shall
    the circling glory glow,
As more and more are taught of God
    that mighty Love to know.

5. O let our adoration
    for all that He hath done,
Peal out beyond the stars of God,
    while voice and life are one;
And let our consecration
    be real, deep, and true;
Oh, even now our hearts shall bow,
    and joyful vows renew.

6. Now onward, ever onward,
    from strength to strength we go,
While grace for grace abundantly
    shall from fulness flow,
To glory's full fruition,
    from glory's foretaste here,
Until His very presence crown
    our happiest New Year.

Frances Ridley Havergal

Sheet music "St. Colomb" from O. Hardwig, ed., *The Wartburg Hymnal.* Chicago: Wartburg Publishing House, 1918, #140, is available at my website, *The Hymns and Carols of Christmas* www.hymnsandcarolsofchristmas.com

New Year's Wishes

March 1858 at Celbridge

Source: Maria V. G. Havergal, ed., *The Poetical Works of Frances Ridley Havergal.* Toronto: Toronto Williard Tract Depot, ND (circa 1880), p. 129.

A PEARL-STREWN pathway of untold gladness,
Flecked by no gloom, by no weary sadness,
    Such be the year to thee !
A crystal rivulet, sunlight flinging,
Awakening blossoms, and joyously singing
    Its own calm melody.

A symphony soft, and sweet, and low,
Like the gentlest music the angels know
    In their moments of deepest joy ;
'Mid earth's wild clamour thy spirit telling
Of beauty and holiness, upward swelling,
    And mingling with the sky.

A radiant, fadeless Eden flower,
Unfolding in loveliness hour by hour,
    Like a wing-veiled seraph's face ;
Such be the opening year to thee,
Shrouded though all its moments be,
    Unknown as the bounds of space.

Blessings unspoken this year be thine !
Each day in its rainbow flight entwine
        New gems in thy joy-wreathed crown ;
May each in the smile of Him be bright,
Who is changeless Love and unfading Light,
Till the glory seem to thy trancèd sight
        As heaven to earth come down.

Candlemas Day

Candlemas is celebrated February 2.

Feb. 1, 1869 at Leamington

Source: Maria V. G. Havergal, ed., *The Poetical Works of Frances Ridley Havergal.* Toronto: Toronto Williard Tract Depot, ND (circa 1880), pp. 650-651.

YES, take the greenery away
That smiled to welcome Christmas Day,
Untwine the drooping ivy spray.

The holly leaves are dusty all,
Whose glossy darkness robed the wall,
And one by one the berries fall.

Take down the yew, for with a touch
The leaflets drop, as wearied much
With light and song, unused to such.

Poor evergreens ! Why proudly claim
The glory of your lovely name,
So soon meet only for the flame ?

Another Christmas Day will show
Another green and scarlet glow,
A fresh array of mistletoe.

And this new beauty, arch or crown,
Will stiffen, gather dust, grow brown,
And in its turn be taken down.

To-night the walls will seem so bare !
Ah, well ! look out, look up, for there
The Christmas stars are always fair.

They will be shining just as clear
Another and another year,
O'er all our darkened hemisphere.

So Christmas mirth has fleeted fast,
The songs of time can never last,
And all is buried with the past.

But Christmas love and joy and peace
Shall never fade and never cease,
Of God's goodwill the rich increase.

Mary's Birthday

Written July, 1850 at Oakhampton
The Nativity of Mary is celebrated on September 8.

Source: Maria V. G. Havergal, ed., *The Poetical Works of Frances Ridley Havergal*. Toronto: Toronto Williard Tract Depot, ND (circa 1880), pp. 88-90.

S HE is at rest,
    In God's own presence blest,
Whom, while with us, this day we loved to greet
    Her birthdays o'er,
    She counts the years no more ;
Time's footfall is not heard along the golden street.

    When we would raise
    A hymn of birthday praise,
The music of our hearts is faint and low ;
    Fear, doubt, and sin
    Make dissonance within ;
And pure soul-melody no child of earth may know.

    That strange ' new song,'
    Amid a white-robed throng,
Is gushing from her harp in living tone ;
    Her seraph voice,
    Tuned only to rejoice,
Floats upward to the emerald-arched throne. [1]

---

1. Rev. iv. 3.

No passing cloud
Her loveliness may shroud,
The beauty of her youth may never fade ;
No line of care
Her sealed brow may wear,
The joy-gleam of her eye no dimness e'er may shade.

No stain is there
Upon the robes they wear,
Within the gates of pearl which she hath passed ;
Like woven light,
All beautiful and bright,
Eternity upon those robes no shade may cast.

No sin-born thought
May in that home be wrought,
To trouble the clear fountain of her heart ;
No tear, no sigh,
No pain, no death, be nigh
Where she hath entered in,
no more, to ' know in part.'

Her faith is sight,
Her hope is full delight,
The shadowy veil of time is rent in twain :
Her untold bliss
What thought can follow this !
To her to live was Christ, to die indeed is gain.

Victorian Visions

Her eyes have seen
The King, no veil between,
In blood-dipped vesture gloriously arrayed :
No earth-breathed haze
Can dim that rapturous gaze ;
She sees Him face to face on whom her guilt was laid.

A little while,
And they whose loving smile
Had melted 'neath the touch of lonely woe,
Shall reach her home,
Beyond the star-built dome ;
Her anthem they shall swell,
her joy they too shall know.

Here Ends

The Christmas Poems
Of
Frances Ridley Havergal

Christiana Georgina Rossetti

1830-1894

Christmas Poetry

Selected From

The Poetical Works of Christina Georgina Rossetti,
with a Memoir and Notes

William Michael Rossetti

London: Macmillan, 1904

C hristiana Rossetti was the fourth child of the Ital-
ian poet Gabriele Rossetti and his wife Frances
Mary Lavinia Polidori. This remarkably artistic and
literary family included her siblings Maria Francesca
(1827), Gabriel Charles Dante (1828), and William
Michael (1829).

According to her brother William, "In childhood she was of a lively, and a somewhat capricious or even fractious, temper; but she was warm-natured, engaging, and a general favourite, considerably prettier than her elder sister Maria. She was by far the least bookish of the family...." But at the age of 15, her health became "obviously delicate." She would continue to be plagued by various ailments until, in 1871, she was stricken with exopthalmic bronchocele (or Dr Graves's disease), described by her brother as "truly most formidable and prostrating;" it also destroyed her good looks and left her with permanent cardiac troubles. In some measure, according to William, this would permanently affect her outlook towards life, leaving her to regard this world as a `valley of the shadow of death.' Nevertheless, as an invalid she had courage, patience, and even cheerfulness.

Baptized into the Anglican Church, she remained firmly devout throughout her life. Her faith had a profound effect on her life. As explained by William:

> Of society (as one uses the term to mean fashionable or quasi-fashionable society) she saw nothing; of amusements practically nothing. She was, I suppose, barely eighteen when she determined never again to enter a theatre, dramatic or operatic; not perhaps that she considered plays and operas to be in themselves iniquitous, but rather that the moral tone of vocalists, actors, and actresses is understood to be lax, and it behooves a Christian not to contribute to the encouragement of lax moralists.

These precepts included her choice of litera-
ture. William wrote: "Any such author as Rabelais[2]
would have been beyond measure repulsive to her —
indeed, heartily despised as well as loathed; and Boc-
caccio,[3] wherever he assimilates to a Rabelaisian side
of things, would have shared the same fate."

She was twice disappointed in love. In her late
teens, she became engaged to the painter James
Collinson, but broke off the engagement due to the
fact that he was a Roman Catholic. Some 16 years
later, another suitor, the author Charles Bagot Cay-
ley, was rejected, also for religious reasons.

As noted above, Christiana went "very little into
society," but she did have a very large circle of
friends, some of whom were among the leading liter-
ary and artistic members of contemporary London
(including many members of the "Pre-Raphaelite
Brotherhood," which also included her brothers). Ac-
cording to William, "In company she was quiet, and
reserved rather than otherwise, but made every now
and then some remark which arrested attention. She
was as a fact extremely shy."

---

2. François Rabelais (c. 1494 - 1553) was a major French
Renaissance writer. "François Rabelais," Wikipedia.
http://en.wikipedia.org/wiki/Fran%C3%A7ois_Rabelais.
3. Giovanni Boccaccio (1313 – 1375), an Italian author and poet,
a friend and correspondent of Petrarch, an important Renaissance
humanist in his own right and author of a number of notable
works including "On Famous Women," the "Decameron" and his
poetry in the vernacular. Source: "Giovanni Boccacio,"
Wikipedia. http://en.wikipedia.org/wiki/Giovanni_Boccaccio.

She traveled abroad twice in her life. In 1861, together with her mother and brother William, she traveled to France, and in 1865, in the same company, she traveled to North Italy.

Although a writer since the age of 7, she was not published until the age of 32 when her collection *Goblin Market and Other Poems* (1862) came into print. Coming two months before the death of Elizabeth Barrett Browning, Christiana was hailed as the natural successor. Well versed in Italian and French, and with a moderate knowledge of German, her brother described her habits of composition as "entirely of the casual and spontaneous kind." Her notebooks were described as "impeccably neat." Her focus was primarily on devotional writing and children's poetry.

After *Goblin Market*, other collections followed regularly, including the following poetic works:

1. Verses, privately printed, 1847.
2. Goblin Market and other Poems, 1862
3. The Prince's Progress and other Poems, 1866
4. Sing-Song, 1872
5. A Pageant and other Poems, 1881
6. Verses, 1893
7. New Poems, 1896

In his Memoir, William provides this listing of her prose works:

1. Commonplace, and other Short Stories, 1870.

2. Annus Domini, a Prayer for each Day of the Year, 1874.

3. Speaking Likenesses, 1874.

4. Seek and Find, 1879.

5. Called to be Saints, 1881.

6. Letter and Spirit, 1883.

7. Time Flies, 1885.

8. The Face of the Deep, a Devotional Commentary on the Apocalypse, 1892.

9. Maude, 1897.

In 1891, she was diagnosed with cancer. An operation was performed in May 1892, but the cancer returned the next year. She took to her bed in August 1894, and died in the early morning of December 29, 1894. She was buried in Highgate Cemetery, London.

This poem, _Portrait_, is a revealing self-view of her life, from _Poems By Christiana Rossetti_ (Boston, 1906):

> She gave up beauty in her tender youth,
>> Gave all her hope and joy and pleasant ways;
>> She covered up her eyes
>>> lest they should gaze
> On vanity, and chose the bitter truth.
> Harsh towards herself,
>> towards others full of truth,
>> Servant of servants, little known to praise,
>> Long prayers and fasts
>>> trenched on her nights and days:

> She schooled herself
> to sights and sounds uncouth,
> That with the poor and stricken
> she might make
> A home, until the least of all sufficed
> Her wants; her own self learned she to forsake,
> Counting all earthly gain but hurt and loss.
> So with calm will she chose and bore the cross,
> And hated all for love of Jesus Christ.

And there is this excerpt from *Autumn* that reflects the depth of her sadness about her two failed loves:

> I dwell alone, – I dwell alone, alone,
> Whilst full my river flows down to the sea,
> Gilded with flashing boats
> That bring no friend to me:
> O love-songs, gurgling from a hundred throats,
> O love-pangs, let me be.

Sources:

- William Michael Rossetti, *The Poetical Works of Christina Georgina Rossetti, with a Memoir and Notes* (London: Macmillan And Co., Limited, 1904). His extensive memoir of his sister's life, too long to include here, provides valuable insights into her life.

- *Poems By Christiana Rossetti.* Boston: Brown, Little and Company, 1906; available at Project Gutenberg as EBook #19188.

- *Goblin Market, The Prince's Progress, and Other Poems*, by Christina Rossetti. 'The World's Classics' published the contents of these two books, together with other poems, in one volume in 1913. Project Gutenberg EBook #16950.

Victorian Visions

Poems for The Advent

Advent

Source: *The Poetical Works of Christina Georgina Rossetti, with a Memoir and Notes* by William Michael Rossetti (1904), Page 148

C ome, Thou dost say to Angels,
To blessed Spirits, 'Come':
'Come,' to the lambs of Thine own flock,
Thy little ones, 'Come home.'

'Come,' from the many-mansioned house
The gracious word is sent;
'Come,' from the ivory palaces
Unto the Penitent.

O Lord, restore us deaf and blind,
Unclose our lips though dumb:
Then say to us, 'I will come with speed,'
And we will answer, 'Come.'

12 December 1851

Advent

Source: _The Poetical Works of Christina Georgina Rossetti, with a Memoir and Notes_ by William Michael Rossetti (1904), Page 157-8

S ooner or later: yet at last
The Jordan must be past;

It may be he will overflow
His banks the day we go;

It may be that his cloven deep
Will stand up on a heap.

Sooner or later: yet one day
We all must pass that way;

Each man, each woman, humbled, pale,
Pass veiled within the veil;

Child, parent, bride, companion,
Alone, alone, alone.

For none a ransom can be paid,
A suretyship be made:

I, bent by mine own burden, must
Enter my house of dust;

I, rated to the full amount,
Must render mine account.

When earth and sea shall empty all
Their graves of great and small;

When earth wrapt in a fiery flood
Shall no more hide her blood;

When mysteries shall be revealed;
All secrets be unsealed;

When things of night, when things of shame,
Shall find at last a name,

Pealed for a hissing and a curse
Throughout the universe:

Then, Awful Judge, most Awful God,
Then cause to bud Thy rod,

To bloom with blossoms, and to give
Almonds; yea, bid us live.

I please Thyself with Thee, I plead
Thee in our utter need:

Jesus, most Merciful of Men,
Show mercy on us then;

Lord God of Mercy and of men,
Show mercy on us then.

Circa 1877

Advent

Source: *The Poetical Works of Christina Georgina Rossetti, with a Memoir and Notes* by William Michael Rossetti (1904), Page 157-8

E arth grown old, yet still so green,
Deep beneath her crust of cold
Nurses fire unfelt, unseen:
Earth grown old.

We who live are quickly told:
Millions more lie hid between
Inner swathings of her fold.

When will fire break up her screen?
When will life burst thro' her mould?
Earth, earth, earth, thy cold is keen,
Earth grown old.

Before 1886

Advent

Source: *The Poetical Works of Christina Georgina Rossetti, with a Memoir and Notes* by William Michael Rossetti (1904), Page 202

This Advent moon shines cold and clear,
These Advent nights are long;
Our lamps have burned year after year
And still their flame is strong.
'Watchman, what of the night?' we cry,
Heart-sick with hope deferred:
'No speaking signs are in the sky,'
Is still the watchman's word.

The Porter watches at the gate,
The servants watch within;
The watch is long betimes and late,
The prize is slow to win.
'Watchman, what of the night?' But still
His answer sounds the same:
'No daybreak tops the utmost hill,
Nor pale our lamps of flame.'

Victorian Visions

One to another hear them speak
The patient virgins wise:
'Surely He is not far to seek' –
'All night we watch and rise.'
'The days are evil looking back,
The coming days are dim;
Yet count we not His promise slack,
But watch and wait for Him.'

One with another, soul with soul,
They kindle fire from fire:
'Friends watch us who have touched the goal.'
'They urge us, come up higher.'
'With them shall rest our waysore feet,
With them is built our home,
With Christ.' – 'They sweet, but He most sweet,
Sweeter than honeycomb.'

There no more parting, no more pain,
The distant ones brought near,
The lost so long are found again,
Long lost but longer dear:
Eye hath not seen, ear hath not heard,
Nor heart conceived that rest,
With them our good things long deferred,
With Jesus Christ our Best.

We weep because the night is long,
We laugh for day shall rise,
We sing a slow contented song
And knock at Paradise.
Weeping we hold Him fast Who wept
For us, we hold Him fast;
And will not let Him go except
He bless us first or last.

Weeping we hold Him fast to-night;
We will not let Him go
Till daybreak smite our wearied sight
And summer smite the snow:
Then figs shall bud, and dove with dove
Shall coo the livelong day;
Then He shall say, 'Arise, My love,
My fair one, come away.'

   2 May 1858

Note from William Michael Rossetti:

"In the annotated copy of her Poems Christina
wrote against this one: 'Liked, I believe, at East
Grinstead' - which one may well credit of the
'Wise Virgins' of that establishment. The greater
part was set to music for Christina's funeral
service at Christ Church, Woburn Square, by
the organist, Mr. [Frank T.] Lowden. I heard the
music sung, and can testify to its beautiful and
touching effect." (page 473)

Editor's Note:

East Grinstead was also the location of Sackville College, an almshouse, of which John Mason Neale was the Warden from 1846 until his death in 1866. Rev. Neale was instrumental in establishing St. Margaret's Sisterhood at East Grinstead. The purpose of the sisterhood was to minister to the bodily and spiritual needs of the sick and suffering poor..." For more information about Rev. Neale, see: http://www.hymnsandcarolsofchristmas.com/Hymns_and_Carols/Biographies/john_mason_neale.htm

I have been unable to locate the sheet music mentioned by Mr. Rossetti for this poem. If I do so, the music will be posted at the web site *The Hymns And Carols Of Christmas*, www.HymnsAndCarolsOfChristmas.com.

Two other of Rossetti's poems were set to music by Frank T. Lowden ("Two Hymns." London: Skeffington and Son, 1895). The hymns were "The Porter Watches at the Gate" and "Lord, Grant Us Grace to Mount." Lowden also created a setting for "All Thy Works Praise Thee, O Lord" (1897).

The poem has been given an SATB setting, with piano or organ accompaniment, by Douglas Brooks-Davies, circa 2000. It is available at the *Choral Public Domain Library* (CPDL), "Advent Anthem," http://www.cpdl.org/wiki/index.php/Advent_Anthem_(The_Advent_moon_shines_cold_and_clear)_(Douglas_Brooks-Davies)

Sunday Before Advent

Source: *The Poetical Works of Christina Georgina Rossetti, with a Memoir and Notes* by William Michael Rossetti (1904), Page 179

The end of all things is at hand. We all
Stand in the balance trembling as we stand;
Or if not trembling, tottering to a fall.
The end of all things is at hand.

O hearts of men, covet the unending land!
O hearts of men, covet the musical,
Sweet, never-ending waters of that strand!

While Earth shows poor, a slippery rolling ball,
And Hell looms vast, a gulf unplumbed, unspanned,
And Heaven flings wide its gates to great and small,
The end of all things is at hand.

Before 1893

Advent Sunday

Source: *The Poetical Works of Christina Georgina Rossetti, with a Memoir and Notes* by William Michael Rossetti (1904), Page 156

BEHOLD, the Bridegroom cometh: go ye out
With lighted lamps and garlands round about
To meet Him in a rapture with a shout.

It may be at the midnight, black as pitch,
Earth shall cast up her poor, cast up her rich.

It may be at the crowing of the cock
Earth shall upheave her depth, uproot her rock.

For lo, the Bridegroom fetcheth home the Bride:
His Hands are Hands she knows, she knows His Side.

Like pure Rebekah at the appointed place,
Veiled, she unveils her face to meet His Face.

Like great Queen Esther in her triumphing,
She triumphs in the Presence of her King.

His Eyes are as a Dove's, and she's Dove-eyed;
He knows His lovely mirror, sister, Bride.

He speaks with Dove-voice of exceeding love,
And she with love-voice of an answering Dove.

Behold, the Bridegroom cometh: go we out
With lamps ablaze and garlands round about
To meet Him in a rapture with a shout.

Before 1886.

Note:

See Matthew 25:1-13, the parable of the Wise and
Foolish Virgins. This is the basis of numerous Advent
poems and hymns.

For Advent

Source: _The Poetical Works of Christina Georgina Rossetti, with a Memoir and Notes_ by William Michael Rossetti (1904), Page 117

S weet sweet sound of distant waters, falling
On a parched and thirsty plain;
Sweet sweet song of soaring skylark, calling
On the sun to shine again;
Perfume of the rose, only the fresher
For past fertilizing rain;
Pearls amid the sea, a hidden treasure
For some daring hand to gain; –
Better, dearer than all these
Is the earth beneath the trees:
Of a much more priceless worth
Is the old, brown, common earth.

Little snow-white lamb, piteously bleating
For thy mother far away;
Saddest sweetest nightingale, retreating
With thy sorrow from the day;
Weary fawn whom night has overtaken,
From the herd gone quite astray;
Dove whose nest was rifled and forsaken
In the budding month of May; –
Roost upon the leafy trees;
Lie on earth and take your ease;
Death is better far than birth:
You shall turn again to earth.

Listen to the never-pausing murmur
Of the waves that fret the shore:
See the ancient pine that stands the firmer
For the storm-shock that it bore;
And the moon her silver chalice filling
With light from the great sun's store;
And the stars which deck our temple's ceiling
As the flowers deck its floor;
Look and hearken while you may,
For these things shall pass away:
All these things shall fail and cease;
Let us wait the end in peace.

Victorian Visions

Let us wait the end in peace, for truly
That shall cease which was before:
Let us see our lamps are lighted, duly
Fed with oil nor wanting more:
Let us pray while yet the Lord will hear us,
For the time is almost o'er;
Yea, the end of all is very near us;
Yea, the Judge is at the door.
Let us pray now, while we may;
It will be too late to pray
When the quick and dead shall all
Rise at the last trumpet-call.

12 March 1849

Christmas Eve

Source: *The Poetical Works of Christina Georgina Rossetti, with a Memoir and Notes* by William Michael Rossetti (1904), Page 158

C HRISTMAS hath darkness
Brighter than the blazing noon,
Christmas hath a chillness
Warmer than the heat of June,
Christmas hath a beauty
Lovelier than the world can show:
For Christmas bringeth Jesus,
Brought for us so low.

Earth, strike up your music,
Birds that sing and bells that ring;
Heaven hath answering music
For all Angels soon to sing:
Earth, put on your whitest
Bridal robe of spotless snow:
For Christmas bringeth Jesus,
Brought for us so low.

    Before 1886

Poems for Christmas

A Christmas Carol

Source: *The Poetical Works of Christina Georgina Rossetti, with a Memoir and Notes* by William Michael Rossetti (1904), Page 217

Before the paling of the stars,
Before the winter morn,
Before the earliest cockcrow
Jesus Christ was born:
Born in a stable,
Cradled in a manger,
In the world His Hands had made
Born a Stranger.

Priest and King lay fast asleep
In Jerusalem,
Young and old lay fast asleep
In crowded Bethlehem:
Saint and Angel, Ox and Ass,
Kept a watch together,
Before the Christmas daybreak
In the winter weather.

Jesus on His Mother's breast
In the stable cold,
Spotless Lamb of God was He,
Shepherd of the Fold:
Let us kneel with Mary Maid,
With Joseph bent and hoary,
With Saint and Angel, Ox and Ass,
To hail the King of Glory.

26 August 1859

Note from William Michael Rossetti:

"This was in the *Lyra Messianica,* [4] 1865, named simply *Before the paling of the stars.* I retain my sister's own title." (page 474)

---

4. Orby Shipley, ed., *Lyra Messianica: Hymns and Verses on the Life of Christ.* London: Longman, Green, Longman,Roberts, and Greene, 1864.

A Christmas Carol

Source: Source: *The Poetical Works of Christina Georgina Rossetti, with a Memoir and Notes* by William Michael Rossetti (1904), Page 117

Thank God, thank God, we do believe,
Thank God that this is Christmas Eve.
Even as we kneel upon this day,
Even so, the ancient legends say
Nearly two thousand years ago
The stalled ox knelt, and even so
The ass knelt full of praise, which they
Could not express, while we can pray.
Thank God, thank God, for Christ was born
Ages ago, as on this morn:
In the snow-season undefiled
God came to earth a little Child;
He put His ancient glory by
To live for us, and then to die.

How shall we thank God? How shall we
Thank Him and praise Him worthily?
What will He have Who loved us thus?
What presents will He take from us?
Will He take gold, or precious heap
Of gems? or shall we rather steep
The air with incense, or bring myrrh?
What man will be our messenger
To go to Him and ask His will?
Which having learned we will fulfil
Though He choose all we most prefer: –
What man will be our messenger?

Thank God, thank God, the Man is found,
Sure-footed, knowing well the ground.
He knows the road, for this the way
He travelled once, as on this day.
He is our Messenger beside,
He is our door, and path, and Guide;
He also is our Offering,
He is the gift that we must bring.
Let us kneel down with one accord
And render thanks unto the Lord:
For unto us a Child is born
Upon this happy Christmas morn;
For unto us a Son is given,
Firstborn of God and Heir of Heaven.

7 March 1849

Note: Also published as *A Christmas Carol (On The Stroke of Midnight)*.

A Christmas Carol

Source: _The Poetical Works of Christina Georgina Rossetti, with a Memoir and Notes_ by William Michael Rossetti (1904), Page 246

In the bleak mid-winter
Frosty wind made moan,
Earth stood hard as iron,
Water like a stone;
Snow had fallen, snow on snow,
Snow on snow,
In the bleak mid-winter
Long ago.

Our God, Heaven cannot hold Him
Nor earth sustain;
Heaven and earth shall flee away
When He comes to reign:
In the bleak mid-winter
A stable-place sufficed
The Lord God Almighty
Jesus Christ.

Enough for Him, whom cherubim
Worship night and day,
A breastful of milk
And a mangerful of hay;
Enough for Him, whom angels
Fall down before,
The ox and ass and camel
Which adore.

Angels and archangels
May have gathered there,
Cherubim and seraphim
Thronged the air,
But only His mother
In her maiden bliss
Worshipped the Beloved
With a kiss.

What can I give Him,
Poor as I am?
If I were a shepherd
I would bring a lamb,
If I were a Wise Man
I would do my part, –
Yet what I can I give Him,
Give my heart.

Before 1872

Note from William Michael Rossetti:

"This was first published in *Scribner's Monthly*, January 1872. It was republished, 1875, in the volume of united poems, being then made to open the series of Devotional Poems." (page 476)

Note:

The best known musical setting of this poem is the tune "Cranham" by Gustav Theodore Holst.

The last stanza is also published separately as "My Gift, From A Christmas Carol" and "A Birthday Gift." See: "A Christmas Carol" http://www.hymnsandcarolsofchristmas.com/Hymns_and_Carols/in_the_bleak_midwinter.htm

A Christmas Carol

For My Godchildren

Source: *The Poetical Works of Christina Georgina Rossetti, with a Memoir and Notes* by William Michael Rossetti (1904), Page 187

The Shepherds had an Angel,
The Wise Men had a star,
But what have I, a little child,
To guide me home from far,
Where glad stars sing together
And singing angels are? –

Lord Jesus is my Guardian,
So I can nothing lack:
The lambs lie in His bosom
Along life's dangerous track:
The wilful lambs that go astray
He bleeding fetches back.

Lord Jesus is my guiding star,
My beacon-light in heaven:
He leads me step by step along
The path of life uneven:
He, true light, leads me to that land
Whose day shall be as seven.

Those Shepherds through the lonely night
Sat watching by their sheep,
Until they saw the heavenly host
Who neither tire nor sleep,
All singing 'Glory glory'
In festival they keep.

Christ watches me, His little lamb,
Cares for me day and night,
That I may be His own in heaven:
So angels clad in white
Shall sing their 'Glory glory'
For my sake in the height.

The Wise Men left their country
To journey morn by morn,
With gold and frankincense and myrrh,
Because the Lord was born:
God sent a star to guide them
And sent a dream to warn.

My life is like their journey,
Their star is like God's book;
I must be like those good Wise Men
With heavenward heart and look:
But shall I give no gifts to God? –
What precious gifts they took!

Lord, I will give my love to Thee,
Than gold much costlier,
Sweeter to Thee than frankincense,
More prized than choicest myrrh:
Lord, make me dearer day by day,
Day by day holier;

Nearer and dearer day by day:
Till I my voice unite,
And I sing my 'Glory glory'
With angels clad in white;
All 'Glory glory' given to Thee
Through all the heavenly height.

    6 October 1856

Note from William Michael Rossetti:

"Christina, from time to time, acted as godmother to various children - mostly, I think, children of poor people in the neighbourhood of Christ Church, Albany Street, Regent's Park. It may be worth noting that this carol was written not at Christmas time, but early in October; and in many instances a reference to dates would show that poems about festivals of the Church, or about seasons of the year, were written at dates by no means corresponding." (page 472)

Note:

This poem is occasionally found under the erroneous title "To My Grandchildren." See: "A Christmas Carol," http://www.hymnsandcarolsofchristmas.com/Hymns_and_Carols/shepherds_had_an_angel.htm

A Hymn For Christmas Day

Source: Rebecca W. Crump, ed., _The Complete Poems
of Christina Rossetti,_ Vol. 3, p. 122
(Penguin, 2001)

The Shepherds watch their flocks by night,
Beneath the moon's unclouded light,
All around is calm and still,
Save the murm'ring of the rill:
When lo! a form of light appears,
And on the awe-struck Shepherds' ears
Are words, of peace and comfort flowing
From lips with love celestial glowing.

Spiritual forms are breaking
Through the gloom, their voices taking
Part in the adoring song
Of the bright angelic throng.
Wondering the Shepherds bend
Their steps to Bethlehem, and wend
To a poor and crowded inn: –
Tremblingly their way they win
To the stable, where they find
The Redeemer of mankind,
Just born into this world of danger,
Lying in an humble manger.

And they spread abroad each word
Which that joyful night they'd heard,
And they glorified the name
Of their gracious God, Who came
Himself to save from endless woe
The offspring of this world below.

Christmas Carols

Source: *The Poetical Works of Christina Georgina Rossetti, with a Memoir and Notes* by William Michael Rossetti (1904), Pages 278-280

1

Whoso hears a chiming for Christmas
    at the nighest
Hears a sound like Angels chanting in their glee,
Hears a sound like palm boughs
    waving in the highest,
Hears a sound like ripple of a crystal sea.

Sweeter than a prayer-bell for a saint in dying,
Sweeter than a death-bell for a saint at rest,
Music struck in Heaven with earth's faint replying,
'Life is good, and death is good, for Christ is Best.'

2

A holy heavenly chime
Rings fulness in of time,
And on His Mother's breast
Our Lord God ever-Blest
Is laid a Babe at rest.

Stoop, Spirits unused to stoop,
Swoop, Angels, flying swoop,
Adoring as you gaze,
Uplifting hymns of praise: –
'Grace to the Full of Grace!'

The cave is cold and strait
To hold the angelic state:
More strait it is, more cold,
To foster and infold
Its Maker one hour old.

Thrilled through with awestruck love,
Meek Angels poised above,
To see their God, look down:
'What, is there never a Crown
For Him in swaddled gown?

'How comes He soft and weak
With such a tender cheek,
With such a soft small hand? –
The very Hand which spann'd
Heaven when its girth was plann'd.

'How comes He with a voice
Which is but baby-noise? –
That Voice which spake with might
"Let there be light" – and light
Sprang out before our sight.

'What need hath He of flesh
Made flawless now afresh?
What need of human heart? –
Heart that must bleed and smart,
Choosing the better part.

'But see: His gracious smile
Dismisses us a while
To serve Him in His kin.
Haste we, make haste, begin
To fetch His brethren in.'

Like stars they flash and shoot,
The Shepherds they salute:
'Glory to God' they sing:
'Good news of peace we bring,
For Christ is born a King.'

3

Lo! newborn Jesus
Soft and weak and small,
Wrapped in baby's bands
By His Mother's hands,
Lord God of all.

Lord God of Mary,
Whom His Lips caress
While He rocks to rest
On her milky breast
In helplessness.

Lord God of shepherds
Flocking through the cold,
Flocking through the dark
To the only Ark,
The only Fold.

Lord God of all things
Be they near or far,
Be they high or low;
Lord of storm and snow,
Angel and star.

Lord God of all men, –
My Lord and my God!
Thou who lovest me,
Keep me close to Thee
By staff and rod.

Lo! newborn Jesus
Loving great and small,
Love's free Sacrifice,
Opening Arms and Eyes
To one and all.

Circa 1887

Note from William Michael Rossetti:

"It is reasonable to suppose that these three carols were written in different years. I am not aware of the correct dates. The first carol was published (in The Century-Guild Hobby-horse) in 1887, and so I give a general date, 'circa 1887.'" (pages 476-477)

Christmas Day

Source: *The Poetical Works of Christina Georgina Rossetti, with a Memoir and Notes* by William Michael Rossetti (1904), Page 158

A baby is a harmless thing
And wins our hearts with one accord,
And Flower of Babies was their King,
Jesus Christ our Lord:
Lily of lilies He
Upon His Mother's knee;
Rose of roses, soon to be
Crowned with thorns on leafless tree.

A lamb is innocent and mild
And merry on the soft green sod;
And Jesus Christ, the Undefiled,
Is the Lamb of God:
Only spotless He
Upon his Mother's knee;
White and ruddy, soon to be
Sacrificed for you and me.

Nay, lamb is not so sweet a word,
Nor lily half so pure a name;
Another name our hearts hath stirred,
Kindling them to flame:
'Jesus' certainly
Is music and melody:
Heart with heart in harmony
Carol we and worship we.

Before 1886

Christmastide

Source: *The Poetical Works of Christina Georgina Rossetti, with a Memoir and Notes* by William Michael Rossetti (1904), Page 159

L ove came down at Christmas,
Love all lovely, Love Divine;
Love was born at Christmas,
Star and Angels gave the sign.

Worship we the Godhead,
Love Incarnate, Love Divine;
Worship we our Jesus:
But wherewith for sacred sign?

Love shall be our token,
Love be yours and love be mine,
Love to God and all men,
Love for plea and gift and sign.

Before 1886

Editor's Note:

See: "Christmastide"

http://www.hymnsandcarolsofchristmas.com/Hymns_and_Carols/love_came_down_at_christmas.htm

Poems for St. John The Apostle

St. John The Apostle

Source: *The Poetical Works of Christina Georgina Rossetti, with a Memoir and Notes* by William Michael Rossetti (1904), Page 159

Beloved, let us love one another, says St. John,
Eagle of eagles calling from above:
Words of strong nourishment for life to feed upon,
'Beloved, let us love.'

Voice of an eagle, yea, Voice of the Dove:
If we may love, winter is past and gone;
Publish we, praise we, for lo it is enough.

More sunny than sunshine that ever yet shone,
Sweetener of the bitter, smoother of the rough,
Highest lesson of all lessons for all to con,
'Beloved, let us love.'

Before 1886

Note:

The Feast Day of St. John The Apostle is December 27. See: Hymns to St. John The Evangelist at *The Hymns and Carols of Christmas*, www.hymnsandcarolsofchristmas.com

St. John The Apostle

Source: *The Poetical Works of Christina Georgina Rossetti, with a Memoir and Notes* by William Michael Rossetti (1904), Page 159

E arth cannot bar flame from ascending,
Hell cannot bind light from descending,
Death cannot finish life never ending.

Eagle and sun gaze at each other,
Eagle at sun, brother at Brother,
Loving in peace and joy one another.

O St. John, with chains for thy wages,
Strong thy rock where the storm-blast rages,
Rock of refuge, the Rock of Ages.

Rome hath passed with her awful voice,
Earth is passing with all her joys,
Heaven shall pass away with a noise.

So from us all follies that please us,
So from us all falsehoods that ease us,–
Only all saints abide with their Jesus.

Jesus, in love looking down hither,
Jesus, by love draw us up thither,
That we in Thee may abide together.

Before 1893

———————————————————

The Holy Innocents

Source: *The Poetical Works of Christina Georgina Rossetti, with a Memoir and Notes* by William Michael Rossetti (1904), Page 159

THEY scarcely waked before they slept,
They scarcely wept before they laughed;
They drank indeed death's bitter draught,
But all its bitterest dregs were kept
And drained by Mothers while they wept.

From Heaven the speechless Infants speak:
Weep not (they say), our Mothers dear,
For swords nor sorrows come not here.
Now we are strong who were so weak,
And all is ours we could not seek.

We bloom among the blooming flowers,
We sing among the singing birds;
Wisdom we have who wanted words:
Here morning knows not evening hours,
All's rainbow here without the showers.

And softer than our Mother's breast,
And closer than our Mother's arm,
Is here the Love that keeps us warm
And broods above our happy next.
Dear Mothers, come: for Heaven is best.

Circa 1877

Note:

The Feast Day of the Holy Innocents is
December 28. See: The Hymns Of The Holy Innocents
at *The Hymns and Carols of Christmas*,
www.hymnsandcarolsofchristmas.com

The Holy Innocents

Source: *The Poetical Works of Christina Georgina Rossetti, with a Memoir and Notes* by William Michael Rossetti (1904), Page 159

U nspotted lambs to follow the one Lamb,
Unspotted doves to wait on the one Dove;
To whom Love saith, 'Be with Me where I am,'
And lo their answer unto Love is love.

For tho' I know not any note they know,
Nor know one word of all their song above,
I know Love speaks to them, and even so
I know the answer unto Love is love.

Before 1893

The Holy Innocents

Source: *The Poetical Works of Christina Georgina Rossetti, with a Memoir and Notes* by William Michael Rossetti (1904), Page 309

S leep, little baby, sleep;
　The holy Angels love thee,
And guard thy bed, and keep
A blessed watch above thee.
No spirit can come near
Nor evil beast to harm thee:
Sleep, Sweet, devoid of fear
Where nothing need alarm thee.

The Love which doth not sleep,
The eternal Arms surround thee:
The Shepherd of the sheep
In perfect love hath found thee.
Sleep through the holy night,
Christ-kept from snare and sorrow,
Until thou wake to light
And love and warmth to-morrow.

　　1 July 1853

Old And New Year Ditties

Source: *The Poetical Works of Christina Georgina Rossetti, with a Memoir and Notes* by William Michael Rossetti (1904), Pages 190-191

1

New Year met me somewhat sad:
Old Year leaves me tired,
Stripped of favourite things I had,
Baulked of much desired:
yet farther on my road to-day,
God willing, farther on my way.
New Year coming on apace,
What have you to give me?
Bring you scathe or bring you grace,
Face me with an honest face,
You shall not deceive me:
Be it good or ill, be it what you will,
It needs shall help me on my road,
My rugged way to heaven, please God.

13 December 1856

2

Watch with me, men, women, and children dear,
You whom I love, for whom I hope and fear,
Watch with me this last vigil of the year.
Some hug their business,
        some their pleasure scheme;
Some seize the vacant hour to sleep or dream;
Heart locked in heart some kneel and watch apart.

Watch with me, blessed spirits, who delight
All through the holy night to walk in white,
Or take your ease after the long-drawn fight.
I know not if they watch with me: I know
They count this eve of resurrection slow,
And cry 'How long?' with urgent utterance strong.

Watch with me, Jesus, in my loneliness:
Though others say me nay, yet say Thou yes;
Though others pass me by, stop Thou to bless.
Yea, Thou dost stop with me this vigil night;
To-night of pain, to-morrow of delight:
I, Love, am Thine; Thou, Lord my God, art mine.

    31 December 1858

3

Passing away, saith the World, passing away:
Changes, beauty, and youth, sapped day by day:
Thy life never continueth in one stay.
Is the eye waxen dim,
          is the dark hair changing to grey
That hath won neither laurel nor bay?
I shall clothe myself in Spring and bud in May:
Thou, root-stricken, shalt not rebuild thy decay
On my bosom for aye.
Then I answered: Yea.

Passing away, saith my Soul, passing away:
With its burden of fear and hope, of labour and play,
Hearken what the past doth witness and say:
Rust in thy gold, a moth is in thine array,
A canker is in thy bud, thy leaf must decay.
At midnight, at cockcrow, at morning, one certain day
Lo the Bridegroom shall come and shall not delay;
Watch thou and pray.
Then I answered: Yea.

Passing away, saith my God, passing away:
Winter passeth after the long delay:
New grapes on the vine, new figs on the tender spray,
Turtle calleth turtle in Heaven's May.
Though I tarry, wait for Me, trust Me,
          watch and pray:
Arise, come away, night is past and lo it is day,
My love, My sister, My spouse,
          thou shalt hear Me say.
Then I answered: Yea.

          31 December 1860

Note by William Michael Rossetti:

"It will be observed that these three lyrics were written in three several years. They used to be called – *The End of the Year* (1856); *New Year's Eve* (1858); *The Knell of the Year* (1860). I have always regarded this last as the very summit and mountain-top of Christina's work. I will not say, nor indeed think, that nothing besides of hers is equal to it; but I venture to hold that, while she never wrote anything to transcend it in its own line, neither did any one else. The poems depends for its effect on nought save its feeling, sense, and sound; for the verses avoid regularity of the ordinary kind, and there is but one single rhyme throughout. The note is essentially one of triumph, though of triumph through the very grievousness of experience past and present.

"In framing the selection of her Devotional Poems, 1875 and 1890, Christina used to put these Ditties last, followed only by Amen and The Lowest Place. In reading them together, it is natural for her brother to reflect whether they indicate any special occurrences in the years to which they relate. I cannot remember that they do – cannot, for instance, say that in 1856 she was in any express sense 'stripped of favourite things she had'; however, the year 1860 (besides being the year of Dante Gabriel's marriage) was that in which Christina, a few days before she wrote The Knell, attained the age of thirty, and her thoughts as to the transit of years may have been more than ordinarily solemn.

"Her reference to her having 'won neither laurel nor bay' has also its interest. The bay began sprouting soon afterwards, with the appearance, in *Macmillan's Magazine* for February 1861, of the poem *Up-hill*, which at once commanded a considerable share of public attention. It is quite possible that Christina — the most modest of poets, but by no means wanting in the self-consciousness of poetic faculty — though in 1860 that the bay had been kept waiting quite long enough; and it is a fact that, between 24 July 1860, the date of The Lambs of Westmoreland, and 23 March 1861, the date of Easter Even, she wrote no verse whatever except this Knell of the Year. (page 472)

Poems for the Epiphany

Ephiphanytide

Epiphany is celebrated on January 6

Source: *The Poetical Works of Christina Georgina Rossetti, with a Memoir and Notes* by William Michael Rossetti (1904), Page 161

Trembling before Thee we fall down to adore Thee,
  Shamefaced and trembling
    we lift our eyes to Thee:
O First and with the last! annul our ruined past,
Rebuild us to Thy glory, set us free
  From sin and from sorrow
    to fall down and worship Thee.

Full of pity view us, stretch Thy sceptre to us,
Bid us live that we may give ourselves to Thee:
O faithful Lord and true! stand up for us and do,
Make us lovely, make us new, set us free —
  Heart and soul and spirit —
    to bring all and worship Thee.

Before 1893

Epiphany

Source: *The Poetical Works of Christina Georgina Rossetti, with a Memoir and Notes* by William Michael Rossetti (1904), Page 160

L ord Babe, if Thou art He
We sought for patiently,
Where is Thy court?
Hither may prophecy and star resort;
Men heed not their report. –
'Bow down and worship, righteous man:
This Infant of a span
Is He man sought for since the world began!' –
'Then, Lord, accept my gold, too base a thing
For Thee, of all kings King.' –

'Lord Babe, despite Thy youth
I hold Thee of a truth
Both Good and Great:
But wherefore dost Thou keep so mean a state,
Low-lying desolate?' –
'Bow down and worship, righteous seer:
The Lord our God is here
Approachable, Who bids us all draw near.' –
'Wherefore to Thee I offer frankincense,
Thou Sole Omnipotence.' –

'But I have only brought
Myrrh; no wise afterthought
Instructed me
To gather pearls or gems, or choice to see
Coral or ivory.' –
'Not least thine offering proves thee wise:
For myrrh means sacrifice,
And He that lives, this Same is He that dies.' –
'Then here is myrrh: alas, yea woe is me
That myrrh befitteth Thee.' –

Myrrh, frankincense, and gold:
And lo from wintry fold
Good-will doth bring
A Lamb, the innocent likeness of this King
Whom stars and seraphs sing:
And lo the bird of love, a Dove,
Flutters and coos above:
And Dove and Lamb and Babe agree in love: –
Come all mankind, come all creation hither,
Come, worship Christ together.

     Before 1886

All Saints

Source: *The Poetical Works of Christina Georgina Rossetti, with a Memoir and Notes* by William Michael Rossetti (1904), Page 148

They have brought gold and spices to my King,
Incense and precious stuffs and ivory;
O holy Mother mine, what can I bring
That so my Lord may deign to look on me?
They sing a sweeter song than I can sing,
All crowned and glorified exceedingly:
I, bound on earth, weep for my trespassing,–
They sing the song of love in heaven, set free.
Then answered me my Mother, and her voice
Spake to my heart, yea answered in my heart:
'Sing, saith He to the heavens, to earth, Rejoice:
Thou also lift thy heart to Him above:
He seeks not thine, but thee such as thou art,
For lo His banner over thee is Love.'

20 January 1852

Poems for the Presentation

Vigil of the Presentation

Source: _The Poetical Works of Christina Georgina Rossetti, with a Memoir and Notes_ by William Michael Rossetti (1904), Page 172

L ong and dark the nights, dim and short the days,
Mounting weary heights on our weary ways,
Thee our God we praise.
Scaling heavenly heights by unearthly ways,
Thee our God we praise all our nights and days,
Thee our God we praise.

> Before 1893

Note:

February 2 is a busy day in the church calendar. On this date is celebrated _The Purification of the Blessed Virgin_ and _The Feast of the Presentation of Christ in the Temple_. It's common name is _Candlemas,_ for the service of the blessing of candles, representative of the entry into this world of Christ, who is the Light of the World.

Feast of the Presentation

The Feast of the Presentation is February 2

Source: _The Poetical Works of Christina Georgina Rossetti, with a Memoir and Notes_ by William Michael Rossetti (1904), Page 172

O firstfruits of our grain,
Infant and Lamb appointed to be slain,
A Virgin and two doves were all Thy train,
With one old man for state,
When Thou didst enter first Thy Father's gate.

Since then Thy train hath been
Freeman and bondman, bishop, king and queen,
With flaming candles and with garlands green:
Oh happy all who wait
One day or thousand days around Thy gate!

And these have offered Thee,
Beside their hearts, great stores for charity,
Gold, frankincense, and myrrh; if such may be
For savour or for state
Within the threshold of Thy golden gate.

Then snowdrops and my heart
I'll bring, to find those blacker than Thou art:
Yet, loving Lord, accept us in good part;
And give me grace to wait,
A bruised reed bowed low before Thy gate.

Circa 1877

Marian Poetry

The Purification of St. Mary The Virgin

The Feast of the Purification is observed February 2.

Source: *The Poetical Works of Christina Georgina Rossetti, with a Memoir and Notes* by William Michael Rossetti (1904), Page 173

Purity born of a Maid:
Was such a Virgin defiled?
Nay, by no shade of a shade.

She offered her gift of pure love,
A dove with a fair fellow-dove,
A dove with a fair fellow-dove.

She offered her Innocent Child
The Essence and Author of Love;
The Lamb that indwelt by the Dove
Was spotless and holy and mild;
More pure than all other,
More pure than His Mother,
Her God and Redeemer and Child.

Before 1886

Vigil of the Annunciation

Source: *The Poetical Works of Christina Georgina Rossetti, with a Memoir and Notes* by William Michael Rossetti (1904), Page 173

All weareth, all wasteth,
All flitteth, all hasteth,
All of flesh and time:–
Sound, sweet heavenly chime,
Ring in the unutterable eternal prime.

Man hopeth, man feareth,
Man droopeth:– Christ cheereth,
Compassing release,
Comforting with peace,
Promising rest where strife and anguish cease.

Saints waking, saints sleeping,
Rest well in safe keeping;
Well they rest today
While they watch and pray –
But their tomorrow's rest what tongue shall say?

Before 1893

Feast of the Annunciation

Source: *The Poetical Works of Christina Georgina Rossetti, with a Memoir and Notes* by William Michael Rossetti (1904), Page 173

H erself a rose, who bore the Rose,
She bore the Rose and felt its thorn.
All Loveliness new-born
Took on her bosom its repose,
And slept and woke there night and morn.

Lily herself, she bore the one
Fair Lily; sweeter, whiter, far
Than she or others are:
The Sun of Righteousness her Son,
She was His morning star.

She gracious, He essential Grace,
He was the Fountain, she the rill:
Her goodness to fulfil
And gladness, with proportioned pace
He led her steps thro' good and ill.

Christ's mirror she of grace and love,
Of beauty and of life and death:
By hope and love and faith
Transfigured to His Likeness, 'Dove,
Spouse, Sister, Mother,' Jesus saith.

Circa 1877

Note:

The Feast of the Annunciation of the Blessed Virgin
Mary is celebrated March 25 in the Latin rite.

Feast of the Annunciation

Source: *The Poetical Works of Christina Georgina Rossetti, with a Memoir and Notes* by William Michael Rossetti (1904), Page 173

Whereto shall we liken this Blessed Mary Virgin,
Faithful shoot from Jesse's root
        graciously emerging?
Lily we might call her, but Christ alone is white;
Rose delicious, but that Jesus is the one Delight;
Flower of women, but her Firstborn
        is mankind's one flower:
He the Sun lights up all moons
        thro' their radiant hour.
'Blessed among women, highly favoured,' thus
Glorious Gabriel hailed her, teaching words to us:
Whom devoutly copying we too cry 'All hail!'
Echoing on the music of glorious Gabriel.

        Before 1866

Poetry for the Candlemas

A Candlemas Dialogue

Candlemas is celebrated February 2.

Source: *The Poetical Works of Christina Georgina Rossetti, with a Memoir and Notes* by William Michael Rossetti (1904), Page 281

L ove brought Me down: and cannot love make thee
Carol for joy to Me?
Hear cheerful robin carol from his tree,
Who owes not half to Me
I won for thee.'

'Yea, Lord, I hear his carol's wordless voice;
And well may he rejoice
Who hath not heard of death's discordant noise.
So might I too rejoice
With such a voice.'

'True, thou hast compassed death: but hast not thou
The tree of life's own bough?
Am I not Life and Resurrection now?
My Cross, balm-bearing bough
For such as thou.'

'Ah me, Thy Cross! – but that seems far away;
Thy Cradle-song to-day
I too would raise and worship Thee and pray:
Not empty, Lord, to-day
Send me away.'

'If thou wilt not go empty, spend thy store;
And I will give thee more,
Yea, make thee ten times richer than before.
Give more and give yet more
Out of thy store.'

'Because Thou givest me Thyself, I will
Thy blessed word fulfil,
Give with both hands, and hoard by giving still:
Thy pleasure to fulfil,
And work Thy Will.'

      Before 1891

Other Christmastide Poetry

Golden Holly

Source: *The Poetical Works of Christina Georgina Rossetti, with a Memoir and Notes* by William Michael Rossetti (1904), Page 426

C ommon Holly bears a berry
To make Christmas Robins merry: –
Golden Holly bears a rose,
Unfolding at October's close
To cheer an old Friend's eyes and nose.

Circa 1872

Note by William Michael Rossetti:

"This trifle, owing to its association of old and uninterrupted friendship, I was unwilling in 1896 to omit: and I know now that I ought not to have omitted it, for Mr. Swinburne pronounced it an excellent thing. It was addressed to Holman [Holly] Frederic Stephens, then a little boy, son of our constant friend, Frederic George Stephens (one of the seven members of the 'P. R. B.'). Tennyson once saw the child in the Isle of Wight, and pronounced him (not unreasonably) to be 'the most beautiful boy I have ever seen.' Mr. Stephens senior, in sending me the verses at my rest, wrote that they refer 'to H. F. S.'s frequent pet name of "The Golden Holly," given because of the brightness of his long hair, as well as his birthday being on October 31. He had sent a tea-rose to C. G. R.' (see page 492)

Editor's Note:

"P.R.B." refers to "PræRaphaelite Brotherhood." The founders of the Brotherhood were the painters Dante Gabriel Rossetti (1828-1882), William Holman Hunt (1827-1910), John Everett Millais (1829-1896), James Collinson (1825-1881), Frederic George Stephens (1828-1907), sculptor Thomas Woolner (1825-1892), and writer William Michael Rossetti (1829-1919), brother of the painter Dante Rossetti. Christina wrote two poems about the P.R.B. In 1863, concerning her brother William, she wrote:

William Rossetti, calm and solemn,
Cuts up his brethren by the column.

At that time, William Rossetti was the art critic of "The Spectator." William responded: "This joke was not historically true; I upheld, with such vigour as was in me, the cause of the Præraphaelites, and my articles, being at first solitary in that tone of criticism, passed not wholly unobserved."

Hail! Noble Face of Noble Friend

Source: R. W. Crump, ed., *The Complete Poems of Christina Rossetti*, Vol. 3, page 347

Hail, noble face of noble friend! –
Hail, honoured master hand and dear! –
On you may Christmas good descend
And blessings of the unknown year
So soon to overtake us here.
Unknown, yet well known: I portend
Love starts the course, love seals the end.

January Cold Desolate

Source: *The Poetical Works of Christina Georgina Rossetti, with a Memoir and Notes* by William Michael Rossetti (1904), Page 432

January cold desolate;
February all dripping wet;
March wind ranges;
April changes;
Birds sing in tune
To flowers of May,
And sunny June
Brings longest day;
In scorched July
The storm-clouds fly
Lightning torn;
August bears corn,
September fruit;
In rough October
Earth must disrobe her;
Stars fall and shoot
In keen November;
And night is long
And cold is strong
In bleak December.

But Give Me Holly, Bold and Jolly

Source: *The Poetical Works of Christina Georgina Rossetti, with a Memoir and Notes* by William Michael Rossetti (1904), Page 441

A ROSE has thorns as well as honey,
I'll not have her for love or money;
An iris grows so straight and fine
That she shall be no friend of mine;
Snowdrops like the snow would chill me;
Nightshade would caress and kill me;
Crocus like a spear would fright me;
Dragon's-mouth might bark or bite me;
Convolvulus but blooms to die;
A wind-flower suggests a sigh;
Love-lies-bleeding makes me sad;
And poppy-juice would drive me mad: –
But give me holly, bold and jolly,
Honest, prickly, shining holly;
Pluck me holly leaf and berry
For the day when I make merry.

Here Ends

The Christmastide Poems
Of
Christiana Georgina Rossetti

Catherine Winkworth
1827-1878

Christmas Poems

Selected From

Lyra Germanica
First Series: Songs for the Household
1855

Lyra Germanica
Second Series: The Christian Life
1858

The Chorale Book For England
1863

Catherine Winkworth was the foremost 19th century translator of German hymns into English. Her translations, with frequent alterations, are still the most widely used of any from German and are used extensively in many denominational hymnals, especially in Lutheran hymnals published in the United States.

Ms. Winkworth was born in No. 20, Ely Place, Holborn, London, England, on September 13, 1827. In 1829, her parents moved to Manchester while she was two as her father had a silk mill (possibly at Macclesfield). Two of her sisters, Emily and Susanna, were left with their grandmother Winkworth and her daughter, Eliza, at Islington.

When they followed their parents to Manchester they had lessons from the Rev. William Gaskell, minister of Cross Street Chapel, Manchester, and husband of the well-known novelist. Catherine Winkworth lived most of her life in Manchester, England (the notable exception was the year she spent in Dresden, Germany).

For nearly two years from January, 1848, Catherine suffered a period of ill-health. In 1852, she undertook active work among the poor in the newly-established Sunday School & District Visiting Society. She was regarded with extreme affection by the poor, and long after she left the neighborhood, she used to receive occasional letters from them.

During her time in Manchester, Catherine came to know Chevalier Bunsen (Christian Karl Josias Bunsen, 1791-1860), who started Catherine and her sister Susanna in their literary work, and to whom Catherine dedicated her *Lyra Germanica* (First Series).

Bunsen, the German ambassador to England, presented her a copy of *Andachtsbuch,* a German devotional book with German hymns, which opened the treasures of German hymnody to her. She went on to publish two series of *Lyra Germanica,* 1855 and

1858. The first series was 103 translations from Bunsen's *Versuch eines allgemeinen Gesang und Gebetbuchs,* 1833, which went to 23 editions; the second series contained 121 more translations from the same book and was published in 12 editions.

Catherine and Susanna spent most of the winter of 1859 at Malvern owing to illness. Catching a fresh chill, Catherine had to stay on at Malvern till October, when they moved to Westen for a change of air. They arrived home at Alderley in time for Christmas, 1859.

In February 1861, their father was taken ill; this was the beginning of his complete breakdown in health, which obliged him to give up his business, and ultimately led to the family leaving Thornfield, Alderley Edge, and moving to Clifton, a suburb of Bristol, in October 1862. Here, she became active in promoting higher education for women. This interest manifested itself in her translations from German of biographies of two founders of sisterhoods for the poor and the sick: *Life of Pastor Fliedner,* 1861, and *Life of Amelia Sieveking,* 1863. As a result of this work, she was in 1870 made secretary of the Committee to Promote the Higher Education of Women.

Also in 1861, Susanna had a serious illness that left her an invalid for some years. In spite of this ill-health, the sisters continued with their translations of German works and made several visits abroad.

In 1863, she published her *The Chorale Book for England,* which contained some of the earlier translations with their proper chorale tunes. In 1869, she published *Christian Singers of Germany*, which contained the biographies of German hymn writers, together with numerous hymns. More than any other single individual, she helped bring the German chorale tradition to the English speaking world.

According to her niece, Catherine went to Mornix near Geneva in 1878 where she joined her cousin Annie Shaen to help in the care of their nephew Frank Shaen, then an invalid. She arrived on June 17th, and on the 21st they proceeded to Monnetiex in Savoy, France. On the morning of the 1st of July she was suddenly attacked by a pain at the heart, and she died within the hour. A few days later, she was laid to rest in the corner of the churchyard set aside for Protestants. In her memory her friends raised a sum sufficient to endow two "Catherine Winkworth" scholarships for women at the Bristol University College, and also to erect a memorial tablet to her in Bristol Cathedral.

Dr. James Martineau said "Her translations ... are invariably faithful and, for the most part, both terse and delicate; and an admirable art is applied to the management of complex and difficult versification."

"Miss Winkworth," says Dr. John Julian in his *Dictionary of Hymnology*, "although not the earliest of modern translators of German into English, is certainly the foremost in rank and popularity. Her translations are the most widely used of any from that language, and have had more to do with the modern revival of the English use of German hymns than the versions of any other writer."

Catherine Winkworth possessed great intellectual and social gifts, and was unusually talented as a translator of hymns.

Sources:

- Christian Classics Ethereal Library. Additional information from a biographical note about Catherine Winkworth which was appended to a later version (Second Edition, 1961) of *Lyra Germanica* by a niece [That web page has disappeared].

- The Cyberhymnal

- The Hymnuts

- John Julian, *Dictionary of Hymnology.* 1892, 1907.

- Catherine Winkworth, *Lyra Germanica, First Series: Songs of the Household.* London: G. Routledge, 1855.

- Catherine Winkworth, *Lyra Germanica, Second Series: The Christian Life.* London: Longman, Green, Longman, and Roberts, 1858.

- Catherine Winkworth, *The Chorale Book For England.* 1863.

- Catherine Winkworth, *Christian Singers Of Germany.* 1869.

Poems For The Advent

Redeemer Of The Nations, Come

Johann Franck (Frank)

Source: *The Chorale Book For England,* 1863

Redeemer of the nations, come!
Ransom of earth, here make Thy home!
Bright Sun, oh dart Thy flame to earth,
For so shall God in Christ have birth!

Thou comest from Thy kingly throne,
O Son of God, the Virgin's Son!
Thou Hero of a twofold race,
Dost walk in might earth's darkest place.

Thou stoopest once to suffer here,
And risest o'er the starry sphere;
Hell's gates at thy descent were riven,
Thy ascent is to highest Heaven.

One with the Father! Prince of might!
O'er nature's realm assert Thy right,
Our sickly bodies pine to know
Thy heavenly strength, Thy living glow,

Victorian Visions

How bright Thy lowly manger beams!
Down earth's dark vale its glory streams,
The splendour of Thy natal night
Shines through all time in deathless light.

See:

"Redeemer of the Nations Come – Winkworth"
http://www.hymnsandcarolsofchristmas.com/Hymns
 and Carols/redeemer of the nations come3.htm

First Sunday in Advent

The Dawn

Christian Friedrich Richter, 1704

Source: *Lyra Germanica:* First Series, Songs for the
Household, 1855

*The night is far spent, the day is at hand; let us
therefore castoff the works of darkness, and let us put
on the armour of light.* From the Epistle.

O watchman, will the night of sin
    Be never past?
O watchman, doth the tarrying day being
To dawn upon thy straining sight at last?
    Will it dispel
Ere long the mists of sense wherein I dwell?

Now all the earth is bright and glad
    With the fresh morn;
But all my heart is cold and dark and sad:
Sun of the soul, let me behold Thy dawn!
    Come, Jesus, Lord!
Oh quickly come, according to Thy word!

Do we not live in those blest days
    So long foretold,
Where Thou shouldst come
    to bring us light and grace?
And yet I sit in darkness as of old,
    Pining to see
Thy glory; but Thou still art far from me.

Victorian Visions

Long since Thou camest for the light
    Of all men here;
And still in me is nought but blackest night.
Yet Am I Thine, O hasten to appear,
    Shine forth and bless
My soul with vision of thy righteousness!

If thus in darkness ever left,
    Can I fulfil
The works of light, while yet of light bereft?
Or how discern in love and meekness still
    To follow Thee,
And all the sinful works of darkness flee?

The light of reason cannot give
    Life to my soul;
Jesus alone can make me truly live,
One glance of His can make my spirit whole.
    Arise, and shine,
O Jesus, on this longing heart of mine!

Single and clear, not weak or blind,
    The eye must be,
To which Thy glory shall an entrance find;
For if Thy chosen ones would gaze on Thee,
    No earthly screen
Between their souls and Thee must intervene.

Jesus, do Thou mine eyes unseal,
    And let them grow
Quick to discern whate'er Thou dost reveal,
So shall I be deliver'd from that woe,
    Blindly to stray
Through hopeless night, while all around is day.

The Coming of the Day of the Lord

Johann von Rist, 1651

Source: *Lyra Germanica:* First Series, Songs for the Household, 1855

Behold the fig-tree, and all the trees; when they now shoot forth, ye see and know of your own selves that summer is now nigh at hand. So likewise ye, when ye see these things come to pass, know ye that the kingdom of God is nigh at hand. From the Gospel.

A wake, thou careless world, awake!
    The final day shall surely come;
What Heaven hath fix'd Time cannot shake,
    It cannot sweep away thy doom.
Know, what the Lord Himself hath spoken
    Shall come at last and not delay;
    Though heaven and earth shall pass away,
His stedfast word can ne'er be broken.

Awake! He comes to judgment, wake!
    Sinners, behold His countenance
In beauty terrible, and quake
    Condemn'd beneath His piercing glance.
Lo! He to whom all power is given,
    Who sits at God's right hand on high,
    In fire and thunder draweth nigh,
To judge all nations under Heaven.

Awake, thou careless world, awake!
   Who knows how soon our God shall please
That suddenly that day should break?
   We fathom not such depths as these.
Oh guard thee well from lust and greed;
   For as the bird is in the snare,
   Or ever of its foe aware,
So comes that day with silent speed.

The Lord in love delayeth long
   The final day, and grants us space
To turn away from sin and wrong,
   And mourning seek His help and grace.
He holdeth back that best of days,
   Until the righteous shall approve
   Their faith and hope, their constant love;
So gentle us-ward are His ways!

But ye, O faithful souls, shall see
   That morning rise in love and joy;
Your Saviour comes to set you free,
   Your Judge shall all your bonds destroy:
He, the true Joshua, then shall bring
   His people with a mighty hand
   Into their promised father-land,
Where songs of victory they shall sing.

Rejoice! the fig-tree shows her green,
   The springing year is in its prime.
The little flowers afresh are seen,
   We gather strength in this great time;
The glorious summer draweth near,
   When all this body's earthly load,
   In light that morning sheds abroad,
Shall wax as sunshine pure and clear.

Arise, and let us day and night
  Pray in the Spirit ceaselessly,
That we may heed our Lord aright,
  And ever in His presence be;
Arise, and let us haste to meet
  The Bridegroom standing at the door,
  That with the angels evermore
We too may worship at His feet.

See:

"Awake! Thou Careless World, Awake!"
http://www.hymnsandcarolsofchristmas.com/Hymns
_and_Carols/awake_thou_careless_world_awake.htm

Found in a slightly altered version in Catherine
Winkworth, *The Chorale Book For England*, 1863:
"Awake, Thou Careless World, Awake! - Version 2."
http://www.hymnsandcarolsofchristmas.com/Poetry
/awake_thou_careless_world_awake.htm

Third Sunday in Advent

Christ the Deliverer

Paul Gerhardt, 1653

Source: *Lyra Germanica:* First Series, Songs for the
Household, 1855

*And it shall be said in that day, Lo, this is our God; we
have waited for Him, and He will save us: this is the
Lord; we have waited for Him, we will be glad and
rejoice in His salvation.*   From the Lesson.

How shall I meet thee? How my heart
    Receive her Lord aright?
Desire of all the earth Thou art!
    My hope, my sole delight!
Kindle the lamp, Thou Lord, alone,
    Half-dying in my breast,
And make Thy gracious pleasure known
    How I may greet Thee best.

Her budding boughs and fairest palms
    Thy Zion strews around;
And songs of praise and sweetest psalms
    From my glad heart shall sound.
My desert soul breaks forth in flowers,
    Rejoicing in Thy fame;
And puts forth all her sleeping powers,
    To honour Jesus' name.

In heavy bonds I languish'd long,
   Thou com'st to set me free;
The scorn of every mocking tongue —
   Thou com'st to honour me.
A heavenly crown wilt Thou bestow,
   And gifts of priceless worth,
That vanish not as here below
   The fading of the earth.

Nought, nought, dear Lord, had power to move
   Thee from Thy rightful place,
Save that most strange and blessed Love
   Wherewith Thou dost embrace
This weary world and all her woe,
   Her load of grief and ill
And sorrow, more than man can know; —
   Thy love is deeper still.

Oh write this promise in your heart,
   Ye sorrowful, on whom
Fall thickening cares, while joy departs
   And darker grows your gloom.
Despair not, for your help is near,
   He standeth at the door
Who best can comfort you and cheer,
   He comes, nor stayeth more.

Nor vex your souls with care, nor grieve
   And labour longer thus,
As though your arm could ought achieve,
   And bring Him down to us.
He comes, He comes with ready will
   By pity moved alone,
To sooth our every grief and ill,
   For all to Him are known.

Nor ye, O sinners, shrink aside,
  Afraid to see His face,
Your darkest sins our Lord will hide
  Beneath His pitying grace.
He comes, He comes, to save from sin,
  And all its pangs assuage,
And for the sons of God to win
  Their proper heritage.

Why heed ye then the craft and noise,
  The fury of His foes?
Lo, in a breath the Lord destroys
  All who His rule oppose.
He comes, He comes, as King to reign!
  All earthly powers may band
Against Him, yet they strive in vain,
  His might may none withstand.

He comes to judge the earth, and ye
  Who mock'd Him, feel His wrath;
But they who loved and sought Him see
  His light o'er all their path.
O Sun of Righteousness! arise,
  And guide us on our way
To yon fair mansion in the skies
  Of joyous cloudless day.

Fourth Sunday in Advent

Christk the King of All Men

George Weiszel, 1635

Source: *Lyra Germanica:* First Series, Songs for the
Household, 1855

*Rejoice in the Lord alway, and again I say, Rejoice
The Lord is at hand.*

From the Epistle

L ift up your heads, ye mighty gates,
Behold the King of glory waits,
The King of kings is drawing near,
The Saviour of the world is here;
Life and salvation doth He bring,
Wherefore rejoice, and gladly sing
    Praise, O my God, to Thee!
    Creator, wise is Thy decree!

The Lord is just, a helper tried,
Mercy is ever at His side,
His kingly crown is holiness,
His sceptre, pity in distress,
The end of all our woe He brings;
Wherefore the earth is glad and sings
    Praise, O my God, To Thee!
    O Saviour, great Thy deeds shall be!

Oh, blest the land, the city blest.
Where Christ the ruler is confest!
Oh, happy hearts and happy homes
To whom this King in triumph comes!
The cloudless Sun of joy He is,
Who bringeth pure delight and bliss;
    Praise, O my God, to Thee!
    Comforter, for Thy comfort free!

Fling wide the portals of your heart,
Make it a temple set apart
From earthly use for Heaven's employ,
Adorn'd with prayer, and love, and joy;
So shall your Sovereign enter in,
And new and nobler life begin.
    Praise, O my God, be Thine,
    For word, and deed, and grace divine.

Redeemer, come! I open wide
My heart to Thee, here, Lord, abide!
Let me Thy inner presence feel,
Thy grace and love in me reveal,
Thy Holy Spirit guide us on
Until our glorious goal is won!
    Eternal praise and fame
    Be offer'd Saviour, to Thy Name!

Note: Also found in Catherine Winkworth, *The Chorale Book For England,* 1863. See: "Lift Up Your Heads, Ye Mighty Gates."
http://www.hymnsandcarolsofchristmas.com/Hymns and Carols/lift up your heads ye mighty gat.htm

Advent

A Dread Hath Come On Me

Ich steh' in Angst und Pein
Simon Dach, 1640

Source: *The Chorale Book For England,* 1863

A dread hath come on me,
I know not where to flee,
My pow'rs can nought avail me;
My trembling limbs grow weak,
My lips refuse to speak,
My heart and senses fail me:

For thinking on that sound
That once shall pierce the ground
And make its slumb'rers tremble,—
"Arise! the Day of Doom
Is come at last,—is come!
Before the judge assemble!

Ah God! no tempest's shock
That cleaves the solid rock
Could make my spirit shiver
As doth that awful tone;
Were my heart steel or stone
'T would hear that voice and quiver.

Victorian Visions

I eat, or wake, or sleep,
I talk, or smile, or weep,
Yet still that voice of thunder
Is sounding through my heart,—
"Forget not what thou art,
The doom thou liest under!

For daily do I see
How many deaths there be,
How swiftly all things wither;
How sickness fills the grave,
Or fire, or sword, or wave
Is sweeping thousands thither.

My turn will soon be here,
The end is drawing near,
I hear its warning plainly;
Death knocketh at my door
And tells me all is o'er,
And I would fly him vainly.

Ah! who in this my strait
Will be mine Advocate?
Will all things leave me friendless?
My wealth and power are dust,
This Judge is ever just,
His righteous doom is endless.

Lord Jesus Christ! 't is Thou
Alone canst help me now,
But 't was for this Thou camest,
To save us in this hour;—
Then show Thy mercy's power,
For they are safe Thou claimest.

Speak Thou for me! Thou art
The refuge of my heart;
With gladness let me hear Thee;
Bid me to Thee ascend,
Where praise shall never end,
And love shall aye be near Thee.

Editor's Note:

One of a number of poems written during and after the Thirty Year's War (1618-1648), and the accompanying pestilence. Properly speaking, this is a poem for the Second Coming, although it is not uncommon for such poems and hymns to be heard during First Advent as an unsubtle reminder of the consequences of failing to heed the message of salvation found in the (First) Advent. See: "A Dread Hath Come On Me," http://www.hymnsandcarolsofchristmas.com/Hymns_and_Carols/a_dread_hath_come_on_me.htm

Ah! Lord, How Shall I Meet Thee

Paul Gerhardt, 1653

Source: *The Chorale Book For England,* 1863

A h! Lord, how shall I meet Thee,
How welcome Thee aright?
All nations long to greet Thee,
My hope, my sole delight!
Brighten the lamp that burneth
But dimly in my breast,
And teach my soul, that yearneth
To honour such high guest.

Thy Zion strews before Thee
Her fairest buds and palms,
And I too will adore Thee
With sweetest songs and psalms;
My soul breaks forth in flowers
Rejoicing in Thy fame,
And summons all her powers
To honour Jesus' name.

Nought, nought, dear Lord, could move Thee
To leave Thy rightful place
Save love, for which I love Thee;
A love that could embrace
A world where sorrow dwelleth,
Which sin and suffering fill,
More than the tongue e'er telleth;—
Yet Thou couldst love it still!

O ye sad hearts that sicken
With hope deferred, and see
The gloom around you thicken,
The joys ye hoped for flee,—
Despair not, He is near you,
Yea, at the very door,
Who best can help and cheer you,
He will not linger more.

Nor sin shall make you fearful,
Ashamed to see His face,
The contrite heart and tearful
He covers with His grace;
He comes to heal the spirit
That mourneth sin-oppressed,
And raise us to inherit
With Him our proper rest.

Victorian Visions

He comes to judge the nations,
A terror to His foes,
A light of consolations
And blessed hope to those
Who love the Lord's appearing:
O glorious Sun, now come,
Send forth Thy beams of cheering
And guide us safely home!

See:
"Ah! Lord, How Shall I Meet Thee"
http://www.hymnsandcarolsofchristmas.com/Hymns
_and_Carols/ah_lord_how_shall_i_meet_thee.htm

The Heart Longing for the Inner Advent

Paul Gerhardt, 1653

Source: *Lyra Germanica:* Second Series, The Christian Life, 1858.

W herefore dost Thou longer tarry,
  Blessed of the Lord, afar?
Would it were Thy will to enter
  To my heart, O Thou my Star,
Thou my Jesus, Fount of power,
Helper in the needful hour!
Sharpest wounds my heart is feeling,
Touch them, Saviour, with Thy healing!

For I shrink beneath the terrors
  Of the law's tremendous sway;
All my countless crimes and errors
  Stand before me night and day.
Oh the heavy, fearful load
Of the righteous wrath of God!
Oh the awful voice of thunder
Cleaving heart and soul asunder!

Victorian Visions

While the foe my soul is telling,
    "There is grace no more for thee,
Thou must make thy endless dwelling
    In the pains that torture me."
Yes, and keener still thy smart,
Conscience, in my anguished heart,
By thy venomed tooth tormented,
Long-past sins are sore repented.

Would I then, to soothe my sorrow,
    And my pain awhile forget,
From the world a comfort borrow,
    I but sink the deeper yet,
She hath comforts that but grieve,
Joys that stinging memories leave,
Helpers that my heart are breaking,
Friends that do but mock its aching.

All the world can give is cheating,
    Strengthless all, and merely nought;
Have I greatness, it is fleeting;
    Have I riches, are they aught
But a heap of glittering earth?
Pleasure? Little is it worth
When it brings no joy or laughter
That we shall not rue hereafter.

All delight, all consolation
    Lies in Thee, Lord Jesus Christ,
Feed my soul with Thy salvation,
    O thou Bread of Life unpriced.
Blessed Light, within me glow,
Ere my heart breaks in its woe;
Oh refresh me and uphold me,
Jesus, come, let me behold Thee.

Joy, my soul, for He hath heard thee,
   He will come and enter in;
Lo! He turns and draweth toward thee,
   Let thy welcome-song begin;
Oh prepare thee for such guest,
Give thee wholly to Thy rest,
With an open'd heart adore Him,
Pour thy griefs and fears before Him.

Thy misdeeds are thine no longer,
   He hath cast them in the sea,
And the love of God shall conquer
   All the strength of sin in thee.
Christ is victor in the field,
Mightiest wrong to Him must yield,
He with blessing will exalt thee
O'er whatever would assault thee.

What would seem to hurt or shame thee
   Shall but work thy good at last;
Since that Christ hath deign'd to claim thee,
   And His truth stands ever fast;
And if thine can but endure,
There is nought so fixed and sure,
As that thou shalt hymn His praises
In the happy heavenly places.

Comfort, Comfort Ye My People

Johannes Olearius, 1671

Source: _The Chorale Book For England,_ 1863

Comfort, comfort ye my people,
    Speak ye peace, thus saith our God;
Comfort those who sit in darkness,
    Mourning 'neath their sorrows' load;
Speak ye to Jerusalem
Of the peace that waits for them,
Tell her that her sins I cover,
And her warfare now is over.

Yea, her sins our God will pardon,
    Blotting out each dark misdeed;
All that well deserved His anger
    He will no more see nor heed.
She hath suffer'd many a day,
Now her griefs have passed away,
God will change her pining sadness
Into ever-springing gladness.

For Elijah's voice is crying
    In the desert far and near,
Bidding all men to repentance,
    Since the kingdom now is here.
Oh that warning cry obey,
Now prepare for God a way;
Let the valleys rise to meet Him,
And the hills bow down to greet Him.

Make ye straight what long was crooked,
  Make the rougher places plain,
Let your hearts be true and humble,
  As befits His holy reign;
For the glory of the Lord
Now o'er earth is shed abroad,
And all flesh shall see the token
That His Word is never broken.

Note:
  Winkworth includes this poem under the
heading of "St. John The Baptist." See: "Comfort,
Comfort Ye My People"
http://www.hymnsandcarolsofchristmas.com/Hymns
 and Carols/comfort comfort ye my people1.htm

Let The Earth
Now Praise The Lord

Heinrich Held, 1643

Source: *The Chorale Book For England,* 1863

L et the earth now praise the Lord,
Who hath truly kept His word,
And the sinner's help and Friend
Now at last to us doth send.

What the fathers most desired,
What the prophets' heart inspired,
What they long'd for many a year,
Stands fulfill'd in glory here.

Abram's promised great reward,
Zion's Helper, Jacob's Lord;
Him of twofold race behold,
Truly come, as long foretold.

Welcome, O my Saviour, now!
Hail! my portion, Lord, art Thou!
Here too in my heart, I pray,
Oh prepare Thyself a way.

Catherine Winkworth

Enter, King of Glory, in!
Purify the wastes of sin
As Thou hast so often done;
It belongs to Thee alone.

As Thy coming was in peace,
Noiseless, full of gentleness,
Let the same mind dwell in me
That was ever found in Thee.

Bruise for me the serpent's head,
That, set free from doubt and dread,
I may cleave to Thee in faith,
Safely kept through life and death!

And when Thou dost come again
As a glorious King to reign,
I with joy may see Thy face,
Freely ransom'd by Thy grace.

See:
"Let the Earth Now Praise the Lord"
http://www.hymnsandcarolsofchristmas.com/Hymns
_and_Carols/let_the_earth_now_praise_the_lor.htm

Once He Came In Blessing

Michael Weiss, 1531

Source: *The Chorale Book For England,* 1863

Once he came in blessing,
All our ills redressing,
Came in likeness lowly,
Son of God most holy,
Bore the cross to save us,
Hope and freedom gave us.

Still He comes within us,
Still His voice would win us
From the sins that hurt us;
Would to Truth convert us
From our foolish errors,
Ere He comes in terrors.

Thus if thou hast known Him,
Not ashamed to own Him,
Nor dost love Him coldly,
But wilt trust Him boldly,
He will now receive thee,
Heal thee, and forgive thee.

But through many a trial,
Deepest self-denial,
Long and brave endurance,
Must thou win assurance
That His own He makes thee,
And no more forsakes thee.

He who thus endureth
Bright reward secureth;
Come then, O Lord Jesus,
From our sins release us.
Let us here confess Thee,
Till in heaven we bless Thee.

See:
"Once He Came in Blessing"
http://www.hymnsandcarolsofchristmas.com/Hymns
_and_Carols/once_he_came_in_blessing.htm

The Deliverer

Johann von Rist, 1651

Source: *Lyra Germanica:* Second Series, The Christian
Life, 1858

A rise, the kingdom is at hand,
　　The king is drawing nigh;
Arise with joy, O faithful band,
　　To meet the Lord most high!
　　Ye Christians, hasten forth,
With holy ardours greet your King,
And glad Hosannas to Him sing,
　　Nought else your love is worth.

Look up, ye drooping hearts, to-day!
　　The King is very near,
O cast your griefs and fears away,
　　For lo! your Help is here;
　　And comfort rich and sweet
In many a place for us is stored,
Where in His sacraments and word
　　Our Saviour we can meet.

Look up, ye souls weigh'd down with care!
　The Sovereign is not far.
Look up, faint hearts, from your despair,
　Behold the Morning Star!
　The Lord is with us now,
Who shall the sinking spirit feed
With strength and comfort at its need,
　To whom e'en Death shall bow.

Hope, O ye broken hearts, at last!
　The King comes on in might,
He loved us in the ages past
　When we sat wrapp'd in night;
　Now are our sorrows o'er,
And fear and wrath to joy give place,
Since God hath made us in His grace
　His children evermore.

O rich the gifts Thou bringest us,
　Thyself made poor and weak;
O love beyond compare that thus
　Can foes an sinner seek!
　For this to Thee alone
We raise on high a gladsome voice,
And evermore with thanks rejoice
　Before Thy glorious throne.

Note: Also found in Catherine Winkworth, *The Chorale Book For England*, 1863. See: "Arise The Kingdom Is At Hand"
http://www.hymnsandcarolsofchristmas.com/Hymns and Carols/arise the kingdom is at hand.htm

The Dayspring from on High

Johann Franck (Frank), 1653

Source: *Lyra Germanica:* Second Series, The Christian
Life, 1858

Ye heavens, oh haste your dews to shed
Ye clouds, rain gladness on our head,
Thou earth, behold the time of grace,
And blossom forth in righteousness!

O living Sun, with joy break forth,
And pierce the gloomy clefts of earth:
Behold, the mountains melt away
Like wax beneath Thine ardent ray!

O Life-dew of the Churches, come,
And bid this arid desert bloom!
The sorrows of Thy people see,
And take our human flesh on Thee.

Refresh the parch'd and drooping mind,
The broken limb in mercy bind,
Us sinners from our guilt release,
And fill us with Thy heavenly peace.

O wonder! night no more is night!
Comes then at last the long'd for light?
Ah yes, Thou shinest, O true Sun,
In whom are God and man made one!

Note:

Also found in Catherine Winkworth, *The Chorale Book For England*, 1863. See: "Ye Heavens, Oh Haste Your Dews To Shed" http://www.hymnsandcarolsofchristmas.com/Hymns_and_Carols/ye_heavens_oh_haste_your_dews_to.htm

The New Year

August Hermann Francke, 1691

Source: *Lyra Germanica:* Second Series, The Christian
Life, 1858

*Composed on his journey to Gotha after his unjust
expulsion from Erfurt; as we are told in the oration
delivered at his grave, "in the full experience of the
unspeakable consolations of the Holy Spirit."*

Thank God that towards eternity
      Another step is won!
Oh longing turns my heart to Thee
      As Time flows slowly on,
Thou Fountain whence my life is born,
Whence those rich streams of grace are drawn
      That through my being run!

I count the hours, the days, the years,
      That stretch in tedious line,
Until, O Life, that hour appears,
      When, at Thy touch divine,
Whate'er is mortal now in me
Shall be consumed for aye in Thee,
      And deathless life be mine.

So glows Thy love within this frame,
   That, touch'd with keenst fire,
My whole soul kindles in the flame
   Of one intense desire,
To be in Thee, and Thou in me,
And e'en while yet on earth to be
   Still pressing closer, nigher!

Oh that I soon might Thee behold!
   I count the moments o'er;
Ah come, ere yet my heart grows cold
   And cannot call Thee more!
Come in Thy glory, for Thy bride
Hath girt her for the holy-tide,
   And waiteth at the door.

And since Thy Spirit sheds abroad
   The oil of grace in me,
And Thou art inly near me, Lord,
   And I am lost in Thee,
So shines in me the Living Light,
And steadfast burns my lamp and bright,
   To greet Thee joyously.

Come! is the voice, then, of Thy Bride,
   She loudly prays Thee come!
With faithful heart she long hath cried,
   Come quickly, Jesus, come!
Come, O my Bridegroom, Lamb of God,
Thou knowest I am Thine, dear Lord;
   Come down and take me home.

Victorian Visions

Yet be the hour that none can tell
    Left wholly to Thy choice,
Although I know Thou lov'st it well,
    That I with heart and voice
Should bid Thee come, and from this day
Care but to meet Thee on Thy way,
    And at Thy sight rejoice!

I joy that from Thy love divine
    No power can part me now,
That I may dare to call Thee mine,
    My Friend, my Lord, avow,
That I, O prince of Life, shall be
Made wholly one in heaven with Thee;
    My portion, Lord, art Thou!

And therefore do my thanks o'erflow,
    That one more year is gone,
And of this Time, so poor, so slow,
    Another step is won;
And with a heart that may not wait
Toward yonder distant golden gate
    I journey gladly on.

And when the wearied hands grow weak,
    And wearied knees give way,
To sinking faith, oh quickly speak,
    And make Thine arm my stay;
That so my heart drink in new strength,
And I speed on, nor feel the length
    Nor steepness of the way.

Then on, my soul, with fearless faith,
  Let nought thy terror move;
Nor aught that earthly pleasure faith
  E'er tempt thy steps to rove;
If slow thy course seem o'er the waste,
Mount upwards with the eagles' haste,
  On wings of tireless love.

O Jesus, all my soul hath flown
  Already up to Thee,
For Thou, in whom is love alone,
  Hast wholly conquered'd me.
Farewell, ye phantoms, day and year,
Eternity is round me here,
  Since, Lord, I live in Thee.

Note:

The line "And Thou art *inly* near me, Lord" was compared against an 1858 edition of *Lyra Germanica* (p. 29). It is correct.

Thou Virgin Soul!

Franz Joachim Buhrmeister

Source: _The Chorale Book For England,_ 1863

Thou virgin soul! O thou
   The crown of woman's story,
Thy Joseph's bliss and glory,
Thy kinswoman thou seekest now,
   There thy faith to cheer and stir
   Through what God hath wrought for her.

My faith, alas! Is week,
   And where it sees not plainly
   It strives to grasp but vainly,
And scarcely cares new strength to seek;
   Seeing now what God can do,
   May my faith grow stronger too!

Thou Pearl of women, here
   Hast to His will resign'd thee,
   Thou wilt not look behind thee;
Thy tender heart, towards one so dear
   To thy friends, doth warmly glow,
   Loving service fain would show.

God! I lament to Thee,
   My will towards good is idle,
   And yet I scarce can bridle
Its sinful impulses in me;
   May my course hereafter prove
   Rich in good works and in love!

At last thou goes forth,
　Most loving soul and fairest,
　With thee thy Lord thou bearest,
The Father's Word comes down to earth.
　Happy thou! That He will be
　Thus companion unto thee.

The world is such a place,
　Where we are pilgrims only,
　And we must fear, if lonely
We meet the end that comes apace.
　Jesus! Let me then by faith
　Walk with Thee through life and death!

Note:
　　Winkworth includes this poem under the heading of "Annunciation."

Wake, Awake, For Night Is Flying

Philip Nicolai, 1598

Source: *The Chorale Book For England,* 1863

Wake, awake, for night is flying,
The watchmen on the heights are crying;
Awake, Jerusalem, at last!
Midnight hears the welcome voices,
And at the thrilling cry rejoices:
Come forth, ye virgins, night is past!
The Bridegroom comes, awake,
Your lamps with gladness take;
Hallelujah!
And for His marriage-feast prepare,
For ye must go to meet Him there.

Zion hears the watchmen singing,
And all her heart with joy is springing,
She wakes, she rises from her gloom;
For her Lord comes down all-glorious,
The strong in grace, in truth victorious,
Her Star is risen, her Light is come!
Ah come, Thou blessed Lord,
O Jesus, Son of God,
Hallelujah!
We follow till the halls we see
Where Thou hast bid us sup with Thee!

Now let all the heavens adore Thee,
And men and angels sing before Thee,
With harp and cymbal's clearest tone;
Of one pearl each shining portal,
Where we are with the choir immortal
Of angels round Thy dazzling throne;
Nor eye hath seen, nor ear
Hath yet attain'd to hear
What there is ours,
But we rejoice, and sing to Thee
Our hymn of joy eternally.

Note:
　　Winkworth includes this poem under the heading of "The Life To Come." See: "Wake, Awake, For Night Is Flying"
http://www.hymnsandcarolsofchristmas.com/Hymns_and_Carols/wake_awake_for_night_is_flying.htm

Ye Sons Of Men, In Earnest

Valentin Thilo, 1642

Source: *The Chorale Book For England,* 1863

Ye sons of men, in earnest
    Prepare your hearts within,
The wondrous Conqu'ror cometh,
    Whose power can save from sin,
Whom God in grace alone
    Hath promised long to send us,
To lighten and befriend us,
    And make His mercy known.

Oh set your ways in order
    When such a guest is nigh;
Make plain the paths before Him
    That now deserted lie.
Forsake what He doth hate,
    Exalt the lowly valleys,
Bring down all pride and malice,
    And make the crooked straight.

The heart that's meek and lowly
    Is highest with our God;
The heart now proud and lofty
    He humbles with His rod;
The heart that's unenticed
    By sin, and fears to grieve Him,
Is ready to receive Him,
    To such comes Jesus Christ.

Twas thus St. John hath taught us,
   'Twas thus he preach'd of yore;
And they will feel God's anger
   Who list not to his lore.
Ah God! now let his voice
   To Thy true service win us,
That Christ may come within us,
   And we in Him rejoice!

Note:
      Winkworth includes this poem under the heading of "St. John The Baptist." See: "Ye Sons Of Men, In Earnest"
http://www.hymnsandcarolsofchristmas.com/Hymns_and_Carols/ye_sons_of_men_in_earnest.htm

Poems For Christmas

A Carol

For Christmas Eve

Martin Luther (_"Written for his little son Hans."_), 1540

Source: _Lyra Germanica:_ First Series, Songs for the Household, 1855

Behold, I bring you good tidings of great joy, which shall be to all people.

Luke ii, 10

From heaven above to earth I come
To bear good news to every home;
Glad tidings of great joy I bring,
Whereof I now will say and sing:

To you this night is born a child
Of Mary, chosen mother mild;
This little child, of lowly birth,
Shall be the joy of all your earth.

'Tis Christ our God who far from high
Hath heard your sad and bitter cry;
Himself will your Salvation be,
Himself from sin will make you free.

He brings those blessings, long ago
Prepared by God for all below;
Henceforth His kingdom open stands
To you, as to the angel bands.

These are the tokens ye shall mark,
The swaddling clothes and manger dark;
There shall ye find the young child laid,
By whom the heavens and earth were made.

Now let us all with gladsome cheer
Follow the shepherds, and draw near
To see this wondrous gift of God
Who hath His only Son bestow'd.

Give heed, my heart, lift up thine eyes!
Who is it in yon manger lies?
Who is this child so young and fair?
The blessed Christ-child lieth there.

Welcome to earth, Thou noble guest,
Through whom e'en wicked men are blest!
Thou com'st to share our misery,
What can we render, Lord, to Thee!

Ah, Lord, who hast created all,
How hast Thou made Thee week and small,
That Thou must choose Thy infant bed
Where ass and ox but lately fed!

Were earth a thousand times as fair,
Beset with gold and jewels rare,
She yet were far too poor to be
A narrow cradle, Lord, for Thee.

For velvets soft and silken stuff
Thou hast but hay and straw so rough,
Whereon Thou King, so rich and great,
As 'twere Thy heaven, art throned in state.

Thus hath it pleas'd Thee to make plain
The truth to us poor fools and vain,
That this world's honour, wealth and might
Are nought and worthless in Thy sight.

Ah! dearest Jesus, Holy Child,[5]
Make Thee a bed, soft, undefiled,
Within my heart, that it may be
A quiet chamber kept for Thee.

My heart for very joy doth leap,
My lips no more can silence keep;
I too must sing with joyful tongue
That sweetest ancient cradle-song —

Glory to God in highest Heaven
Who unto man His Son hath given!
While angels sing with pious mirth
A glad New Year to all the earth.

Note:

Also found in Catherine Winkworth, _The Chorale Book For England_, 1863. See: "From Heaven Above To Earth I Come."
http://www.hymnsandcarolsofchristmas.com/Hymns_and_Carols/from_heaven_above_winkworth.htm

For notes and other translations, see "Vom Himmel hoch da komm ich her."
http://www.hymnsandcarolsofchristmas.com/Hymns_and_Carols/NonEnglish/vom_himmel_hoch_da_komm_ich_her.htm

---

5. The last three verses are occasionally sung as a separate hymn.

The Word Made Flesh

For Christmas Day

Laurentius Laurenti, 1700

Source: *Lyra Germanica:* First Series, Songs for the
Household, 1855

And the Word was made flesh, and dwelt among us.

From the Gospel

O Thou essential Word,
   Who from eternity
Didst dwell with God, for Thou wast God,
   Who art ordain'd to be
The Saviour of our race;
   Welcome indeed Thou art,
Blessed Redeemer, Fount of Grace,
   To this my longing heart!

Come, self-existent Word,
   And speak within my heart,
That from the soul where Thou art heard,
   Thy peace may ne'er depart.
Thou Light that lightenest all,
   Abide through faith in me,
And let me never from Thee fall,
   And seek no guide but Thee.

Why didst Thou leave Thy throne,
   O Jesus, what could bring
Thee to a world where e'en Thine own
   Knew not their rightful King?
   Thy love beyond all thought
   Stronger than Death of Hell,
And my deep woe, this wonder wrought,
   That Thou on earth dost dwell.

Then help me, Lord, to give
   My whole heart unto Thee,
That all my life while here I live
   One song of praise may be.
   Yes, Jesus, form anew
   This stony heart of mine,
And let it e'en in death be true
   To Thee, for ever Thine.

Let nought be left within
   But cometh of Thy hand;
Root quickly out the weeds of sin,
   My cunning foe withstand.
   From Thee comes nothing ill,
   'Tis he doth sow the tares;
Make plain my path before me still,
   And save me from his snares.

Catherine Winkworth

Thou art the Life, O Lord!
Sole Light of Life Thou art !
Let not Thy glorious rays be pour'd
    In vain on my dark heart.
Star of the East, arise!
Drive all my clouds away,
Guide me till earth's dim twilight dies
    Into the perfect day !

The Desire of all Nations

Sunday After Christmas Day

Paul Gerhardt, 1650

Source: *Lyra Germanica:* First Series, Songs for the
Household, 1855

*Behold, A Virgin shall be with child, and shall bring
forth a Son, and they shall call His name Emmanuel,
which being interpreted is, God with us.*

From the Gospel

Thee, O Immanuel, we praise,
The Prince of Life, and Fount of Grace,
The Morning Star, the Heavenly Flower,
The Virgin's Son, the Lord of Power.

With all Thy saints, Thee, Lord, we sing,
Praise, honour, thanks to Thee we bring,
That Thou, O long-expected guest,
Hast come at last to make us blest!

Since first the world began to be,
How many a heart hath long'd for Thee;
Long years our fathers hoped of old
Their eyes might yet Thy Light behold:

The prophets cried; "Ah, would He came
To break the fetters of our shame;
That help from Zion came to men,
Israel were glad, and prosper'd then!"

Now art Thou here; we know Thee now,
In lowly manger liest Thou;
A child, yet makest all things great,
Poor, yet is earth Thy robe of state.

From Thee alone all gladness flows,
Who yet shall bear such bitter woes;
Earth's light and comfort Thou shalt be,
Yet none shall watch to comfort Thee.

All heavens are Thine, yet Thou dost come
To sojourn in a stranger's home;
Thou hangest on Thy mother's breast
Who art the joy of spirits blest.

Now fearless I can look on Thee,
From sin and grief Thou sett'st me free;
Thou bearest wrath, Thou conquerest Death,
Fear turns to joy Thy glance beneath.

Thou art my Head, my Lord Divine,
I am Thy member, wholly Thine,
And in Thy Spirit's strength would still
Serve Thee according to Thy will.

Thus will I sing Thy praises here
With joyful spirit year by year.
And they shall sound before Thy throne,
Where time nor number more are known.

Note:

Also found in Catherine Winkworth, _The Chorale Book For England_, 1863. See: "Thee, O Immanuel, We Praise." http://www.hymnsandcarolsofchristmas.com/Hymns and Carols/thee o immanuel we praise.htm

A Song of Joy at Dawn

For Christmas

Paul Gerhardt, 1651

Source: *Lyra Germanica:* Second Series, The Christian Life, 1858

All my heart this night rejoices,
    As I hear,
    Far and near,
Sweetest angel voices;
"Christ is born," their choirs are singing,
    Till the air
    Everywhere
Now with joy is ringing.

For it dawns, — the promised morrow
    Of His birth
    Who the earth
Rescues from her sorrow.
God to wear our form descendeth,
    Of His grace
    To our race
Here His Son He lendeth:

Victorian Visions

Yea, so truly for us careth,
    That His Son
    All we've done
As our offering beareth;
As our Lamb who, dying for us,
    Bears our load,
    And to God
Doth in peace restore us.

Hark! a voice from yonder manger,
    Soft and sweet,
    Doth entreat,
"Flea from woe and danger;
Brethren come, from all doth grieve you
    You are freed,
    All you need
I will surely give you."

Come then, let us hasten yonder;
    Her let all,
    Great and small,
Kneel in awe and wonder.
Love Him who with love is yearning;
    Hail the Star
    That from far
Bright with hope is burning!

Ye who pine in weary sadness,
    Weep no more,
    For the door
Now is found of gladness.
Cling to Him for He will guide you
    Where no cross
    Pain or loss,
Can again betide you.

Hither come, ye heavy-hearted;
    Who for sin
    Deep within,
Long and sore have smarted;
For the poison'd wounds you're feeling
    Help is near,
    One is here
Mighty for their healing!

Hither come, ye poor and wretched;
    Know His will
    Is to fill
Every hand outstretched;
Here are riches without measure,
    Here forget
    All regret,
Fill your hearts with treasure.

Blessed Saviour, let me find Thee!
    Keep Thou me
    Close to Thee,
Cast me not behind Thee!
Life of life, my heart Thou stillest,
    Calm I rest
    On Thy breast,
All this void Thou fillest.

Thee, dear Lord, with heed I'll cherish,
    Live to Thee,
    And with Thee
Dying, shall not perish;
But shall dwell with Thee for ever,
    Far on high
    In the joy
That can alter never.

Note:

Also found in a slightly shortened version in Catherine Winkworth, *The Chorale Book For England,* 1863. See "All My Heart This Night Rejoices." http://www.hymnsandcarolsofchristmas.com/Hymns and Carols/all my heart this night rejoices 1.htm

We Love Him
For He First Loved Us

For Christmas

Gerhardt Tersteegen, 1731

Source: *Lyra Germanica:* Second Series, The Christian
Life, 1858

Thou fairest Child Divine,
    In yonder manger laid,
In whom is God Himself well pleased,
    By whom were all things made,
On me art Thou bestow'd;
    How can such wonders be!
The dearest that the Father hath
    He gives me here in Thee!

I was a foe to God,
    I fought in Satan's host,
I trifled all His grace away,
    Alas! my soul was lost.
Yet God forgets my sin,
    His heart, with pity moved,
He gives me, Heavenly Child, in Thee;
    Lo! thus our God hath loved!

Once blind with sin and self,
    Along the treacherous way,
That ends in ruin at the last,
    I hasten'd far astray;
Then God sent down His Son;
    For with a love most deep,
Most undeserved, His heart still yearn'd
    O'er me, poor wandering sheep!

God with His life of love
    To me was far and strange,
My heart clung only to the world
    Of fight and sense and change;
In Thee, Immanuel,
    Are God and man made one;
In Thee my heart hath peace with God,
    And union in the Son.

Oh ponder this, my soul,
    Our God hath loved us thus,
That even His only dearest Son
    He freely giveth us.
Thou precious gift of God,
    The pledge and bond of love,
With thankful heart I kneel to take
    This treasure from above.

I kneel beside Thy couch,
    I press Thee to my heart,
For Thee I gladly all forsake
    And from the creature part:
Thou priceless Pearl! lo, he
    By whom Thou'rt loved and known,
Will give himself and all he hath
    To win Thee for his own.

Oh come, Thou Blessed Child,
   Thou Saviour of my soul,
For ever bound to Thee, my name
   Among Thy host enrol.
O deign to take my heart,
   And let Thy heart be mine,
That all my love flow out to Thee,
   And lose itself in Thine.

Let Us All With Gladsome Voice

For Christmas

Anonymous, appears 1682

Source: *The Chorale Book For England,* 1863

L et us all with gladsome voice
Praise the God of heaven,
Let us all with gladsome voice
Praise the God of heaven,
Who to bid our hearts rejoice
His own Son hath given.

Down to this sad earth He comes,
Here to serve us deigning,
Down to this sad earth He comes,
Here to serve us deigning,
That with Him in yon fair homes
We may once be reigning.

We are rich, for He was poor,
Gaze upon this wonder!
We are rich, for He was poor,
Gaze upon this wonder!
Let us praise God evermore,
Here on earth, and yonder!

Look on all who sorrow here,
Lord, in pity bending,
Look on all who sorrow here,
Lord, in pity bending,
Grant us now a glad New Year,
And a blessed ending!

See:
“Let Us All With Gladsome Voice”
http://www.hymnsandcarolsofchristmas.com/Hymns
_and_Carols/let_us_all_with_gladsome_voice.htm

God With Us

For Christmas

Paul Gerhardt

Source: *Lyra Germanica:* Second Series, The Christian
Life, 1858

Blessed Jesus! This
    Thy lowly manger is
The Paradise where oft my soul would feed:
    Here is the place, my Lord,
    Where lies the Eternal Word
Clothed with our flesh, made like to us indeed.

    For He whose mighty sway
    The winds and seas obey,
Submits to serve, and stoops to those who sin;
    The glorious Son of God
    Doth bear the mortal load
Of earth and dust, like us and all our kin.

    For thus, O God Supreme,
    Wilt Thou our flesh redeem,
And rise it to Thy throne o'er every height:
    Eternal Strength, here Thou
    To brotherhood dost bow
With transient things that pass like mists of night.

Thy glory and Thy joy
All woe and grief destroy;
Thou, Heavenly Treasure, dost all wealth restore!
Thou deep and living Well!
Thou great Immanuel
Dost conquer sin and death for evermore!

Then come, whoe'er thou art
O poor desponding heart,
Take courage now, let this thy fears dispel,
That since His Son most dear
Thy God hath given thee here,
It cannot be but God doth love thee well.

How often dost thou think
That thou must surely sink,
That hope and comfort are no more for thee;
Come hither then and gaze
Upon this Infant's face,
And here the love of God incarnate see.

Ah now the blessed door
Stands open evermore
To all the joys of this world and the next:
This Babe will be our Friend,
And quickly make an end
Of all that faithful hearts long time hath vex'd.

Then, earth, we care no more
To seek thy richest store,
If but this treasure will be still our own;
And he who holds it fast,
Till all this life is past,
Our Lord will crown with joy before His throne.

O Rejoice, Ye Christians, Loudly

For Christmas

Christian Keimann, 1656

Source: *The Chorale Book For England,* 1863

Hallelujah, Hallelujah

O h rejoice, ye Christians, loudly,
　For your joy is now begun;
Wondrous things our God hath done;
Tell abroad His goodness proudly,
Who our race hath honour'd thus
That he deigns to dwell with us:
Joy, O joy, beyond all gladness!
Christ hath done away with sadness!
Hence, all sorrow and repining,
For the Son of grace is shining.

See, my soul, thy Saviour chooses
Weakness here and poverty,
In such love He comes to thee,
Nor the hardest couch refuses;
All He suffers for thy good,
To redeem thee by His blood:
Joy, then, joy beyond all gladness!
Christ hath done away with sadness!
Hence, all sorrow and repining,
For the Sun of grace is shining.

Lord, how shall I thank Thee rightly?
I acknowledge that from Thee
Every blessing flows to me.
Let me not forget it lightly,
But to Thee through all things cleave;
So shall heart and mind receive
Joy, yea, joy beyond all gladness!
Christ hath done away with sadness!
Hence, all sorrow, all repining,
For the Sun of grace is shining!

Jesu, guard and guide Thy members,
Fill Thy brethren with Thy grace,
Hear their prayers in every place,
Quicken now life's faintest embers;
Grant all Christians, far and near,
Holy peace, a glad New Year!
Joy, O joy, beyond all gladness!
Christ hath done away with sadness!
Hence, all sorrow, all repining,
For the Sun of grace is shining!

See:
"Oh Rejoice, Ye Christians, Loudly"
http://www.hymnsandcarolsofchristmas.com/Hymns
and Carols/oh rejoice ye christians loudly.htm

Rejoice, Rejoice, Ye Christians

For Christmas

Anonymous, early

Source: *The Chorale Book For England,* 1863

Rejoice, rejoice, ye Christians,
With all your hearts this morn!
O hear the blessed tidings,
"The Lord, the Christ, is born,"
Now brought us by the angels
That stand about God's throne;
Oh lovely are the voices
That make such tidings known.
That make such tidings known.

Oh hearken to their singing,
"This Child shall be your Friend,
The Father so hath will'd it,
That thus your woes should end;
The Son is freely given,
That in Him ye may have
The Father's grace and blessing,
And know He loves to save.
And know He loves to save.

Nor deem the form too lowly
That clothes Him at this hour;
For know ye what it hideth?
'Tis God's almighty power.
Though now within the manger
So poor and weak He lies,
He is the Lord of all things,
He reigns above the skies.
He reigns above the skies.

Sin, Death, and Hell, and Satan
Have lost the victory;
This Child shall overthrow them,
As ye shall surely see;
Their wrath shall nought avail them,
Fear not, their reign is o'er;
This Child shall overthrow them,—
Oh hear and doubt no more.
Oh hear and doubt no more."

See:
    "Rejoice, Rejoice, Ye Christians"
http://www.hymnsandcarolsofchristmas.com/Hymns
_and_Carols/rejoice_rejoice_ye_christians.htm

We Christians May Rejoice To-day

For Christmas

? Gaspar Fugger, +1617

Source: *The Chorale Book For England,* 1863

We Christians may rejoice to-day,
When Christ was born
  to comfort and to save us;
Who thus believes no longer grieves,
For none are lost who grasp the hope He gave us.

O wondrous joy, that God most high
Should take our flesh,
  and thus our race should honour;
A virgin mild hath borne this Child,
Such grace and glory God hath put upon her.

Sin brought us grief, but Christ relief,
When down to earth He came for our salvation;
  Since God with us is dwelling thus,
Who dares to speak the Christian's condemnation?

Then hither throng, with happy song
To Him whose birth and death are our assurance;
  Through whom are we at last set free
From sins and burdens that surpassed endurance.

Yes, let us praise our God and raise
Loud hallelujahs to the skies above us
The bliss bestowed to-day by God,
To ceaseless thankfulness and joy should move us.

Note:

The question mark was Winkworth's. See:
"We Christians May Rejoice Today"
http://www.hymnsandcarolsofchristmas.com/Hymns
_and_Carols/we_christians_may_rejoice_today.htm

Also see "All Christians May Rejoice To-day"
http://www.hymnsandcarolsofchristmas.com/Hymns
_and_Carols/all_christians_may_rejoice_today.htm

Poems For The Feasts of Christmas Week

A Battle Song In Troubled Times

For The Feast of St. Stephen's Day
December 26.

Gustavus Adolphus' Battle-song, Altenburg, 1631

Source: *Lyra Germanica:* First Series, Songs for the Household, 1855

And Stephen, full of faith and power, did great wonders and miracles among the people. ... Then they stirred up the people ... and caught him, and set up false witness against him.

From the Lesson

Fear not, O little flock, the foe
Who madly seeks your overthrow,
　Dread not his rage and power:
What though your courage sometimes faints,
His seeming triumph o'er God's saints
　Lasts but a little hour.

Be of good cheer; your cause belongs
To Him who can avenge your wrongs,
　Let it to Him our Lord.
Though hidden yet from all our eyes,
He sees the Gideon who shall rise
　To save us, and His word.

As true as God's own word is true,
Nor earth nor hell with all their crew
   Against us shall prevail.
A jest and by-word are they grown;
God is with us, we are His own,
   Our victory cannot fail.

Amen, Lord Jesus, grant our prayer!
Great Captain, now Thine arm make bare;
   Fight for us once again!
So shall Thy saints and martyrs raise
A mighty chorus to Thy praise,
   World without end. Amen.

See:

     Hymns to St. Stephen at _The Hymns and Carols of Christmas_, www.hymnsandcarolsofchristmas.com

Christic the Life of the Soul

For The Feast of St. John the Evangelist
December 27

Sinold, 1710

Source: *Lyra Germanica:* First Series, Songs for the
Household, 1855

*If I will that he tarry till I come, what is that to thee?
Follow thou Me.*

From the Gospel

I f Thou, True Life, wilt in me live,
    Consume whate'er is not of Thee;
One look of Thine more joy can give
    Than all the world can offer me.
O Jesus, be Thou mine for ever,
Nought from Thy love my heart can sever,
As Thou hast promised in Thy Word;
    O deep the joy whereof I drink,
    Whene'er my soul in Thee can sink,
And own her Bridegroom and her Lord!

O Heart, that glow'd with love and died,
    Kindle my soul with fire divine;
Lord, in the heart Thou'st won, abide,
    And all in it that is not Thine
O let me conquer and destroy,
Strong in Thy love, Thou Fount of Joy,
Nay be Thou Conqueror, Lord, in me;
    So shall I triumph o'er despair,
    O'er death itself Thy victory share,
Thus suffer, live, and die in Thee.

And let the fire within me move
    My heart to serve Thy members here;
Let me their need and trials prove,
    That I may know my love sincere
And like to Thine, Lord, pure and warm;
For when my soul hath won that form
Is likest to Thy holy mind,
    Then I shall love both friends and foes,
    And learn to grieve o'er others' woes,
Like Thee, my Pattern, true and kind.

The light and strength of Faith, oh grant,
    That I may bring forth holy fruit,
A living branch, a blooming plant,
    Fast clinking to my vine — my root:
Thou art my Saviour, whom I trust,
My Rock, — I build not on the dust, —
The ground of faith, eternal, sure.
    When hours of doubt o'er cloud my mind,
    Thy ready help then let me find,
Thy strength my sickening spirit cure!

And grant that Hope may never fail,
   But anchor'd safely on Thy cross,
Through Thee who art mine All, prevail
O'er every anguish, dread, and loss.
The world may build on what decays,
O Christ, my Sun of Hope, my gaze
Cares not o'er lesser lights to range;
   To Thee in love I ever cleave,
   For well I know Thou ne'er wilt leave
My soul, — Thy love can never change.

Wouldst Thou that I should tarry here,
   I live because Thou willest it;
Or Death should suddenly appear.
   I shall not fear him, Lord, one whit,
If but Thy life still in me live,
If but Thy death me strength shall give,
When earthly life draws near its end;
   To Thee I give away my will,
   In life and death remembering still
Thou wilt my good, O truest Friend.

See:

   Hymns to St. John The Evangelist at _The Hymns and Carols of Christmas,_ www.hymnsandcarolsofchristmas.com

────────────────

The Christlike Heart

The Holy Innocents
December 28

Gerhardt Tersteegen, 1731

Source: *Lyra Germanica:* First Series, Songs for the Household, 1855

Except ye be converted, and become as little children, ye shall not enter into the kingdom of Heaven.

Matt. Xviii, 3

Dear Soul, couldst thou become a child
While yet on earth, meek, undefiled,
Then God Himself were ever near,
And Paradise around thee here.

A child cares nought for gold or treasure,
Nor fame nor glory yield him pleasure;
In perfect trust, he asketh not
If rich or poor shall be his lot.

Little he recks of dignity,
Nor prince nor monarch feareth he;
Strange that a child so weak and small
Is oft the boldest of us all!

He hath not skill to utter lies,
His very soul is in his eyes;
Single his aim in all, and true,
And apt to praise what others do.

Victorian Visions

No questions dark his spirit vex,
No faithless doubts his soul perplex,
Simply from day to day he lives,
Content with what the present gives.

Scarce can he stand alone, far less
Would roam abroad in loneliness;
Fast clinging to his mother still,
She bears and leads him at her will.

He will not stay to pause and choose,
His father's guidance e'er refuse,
Thinks not of danger, fears no harm,
Wrapt in obedience' holy calm.

For strange concerns he careth nought;
What others do, although were wrought
Before his eyes the worse offence,
Stains not his tranquil innocence.

His dearest work, his best delight,
Is, lying in his mother's sight,
To gaze for ever on her face,
And nestle in her fond embrace.

O childhood's innocence! the voice
Of thy deep wisdom is my choice!
Who hath thy lore is truly wise,
And precious in our Father's eyes.

Spirit of childhood! loved of God,
By Jesu's Spirit now bestow'd;
How often have I longed for thee;
O Jesus, form Thyself in me!

And help me to become a child
While yet on earth, meek, undefiled,
That I may find God always near,
And Paradise around me here.

See:

The Hymns Of The Holy Innocents at *The Hymns and Carols of Christmas,* www.hymnsandcarolsofchristmas.com

---

Poems For The New Year
& The Circumcision

A Hymn for New Year's Day

The Circumcision of Christ

Daniel Wülffer, 1648

Source: *Lyra Germanica:* First Series, Songs for the
Household, 1855

*So teach us to number our days, that we may apply
our hearts unto wisdom.*   Psalm xc, 12

E ternity! Eternity!
How long art thou, Eternity!
And yet to thee Time hastes away,
Like as the warhorse to the fray,
Or swift as couriers homeward go,
Or ship to port, or shaft from bow.
Ponder, O man, Eternity!

Eternity! Eternity!
How long art thou Eternity!
For even as on a perfect sphere
End nor beginning can appear,
Even so, Eternity, in thee
Entrance nor exit can there be.
Ponder, O Man, Eternity!

Eternity! Eternity!
How long art thou Eternity!
A circle infinite art thou,
Thy center an Eternal Now,
Never, we name thy outer bound,
For never end therein is found.
Ponder, O Man, Eternity!

Eternity! Eternity!
How long art thou Eternity!
A little bird with fretting beak
Might wear to nought the loftiest peak,
Though but each thousand years it came,
Yet thou wert then, as now, the same.
Ponder, O Man, Eternity!

Eternity! Eternity!
How long art thou Eternity!
As long as God is God, so long
Endure the pains of sin and wrong,
So long the joys of heaven remain;
Oh lasting joy, Oh lasting pain!
Ponder, O Man, Eternity!

Eternity! Eternity!
How long art thou Eternity!
O Man, full oft thy thoughts should dwell
Upon the pains of sin and hell,
And on the glories of the pure,
That both beyond all time endure.
Ponder, O Man, Eternity!

Eternity! Eternity!
How long art thou Eternity!
How terrible art thou in woe,
How fair where joys for ever glow!
God's goodness sheddeth gladness here,
His justice there wakes bitter fear.
Ponder, O Man, Eternity!

Eternity! Eternity!
How long art thou Eternity!
They who lived poor and naked, rest
With God for eve rich and blest,
And love and praise the Highest Good,
In perfect bliss and gladsome mood.
Ponder, O Man, Eternity!

Eternity! Eternity!
How long art thou Eternity!
A moment lasts all joy below,
Whereby man sinks to endless woe,
A moment lasts all earthly pain,
Whereby an endless joy we gain.
Ponder, O Man, Eternity!

Eternity! Eternity!
How long art thou Eternity!
Who ponders oft on thee, is wise,
All fleshly lusts will he despise,
The world finds place with him no more;
The love of vain delights is o'er.
Ponder, O Man, Eternity!

Catherine Winkworth

Eternity! Eternity!
How long art thou Eternity!
Who marks thee well would say to God,
Here judge, smite me with Thy rod,
Here let me all Thy justice bear,
When time of grace is past, then spare!
Ponder, O Man, Eternity!

Eternity! Eternity!
How long art thou Eternity!
Lo, I, Eternity, warn thee,
O Man, that oft thou think on me,
The sinner's punishment and pain,
To them who love their God, rich gain!
Ponder, O Man, Eternity!

The Old Year
Now Hath Pass'd Away
For The New Year

Jakob Tapp, 1603

Source: *The Chorale Book For England,* 1863

The old year now hath pass'd away,
We thank Thee, O our God, to-day,
That Thou hast kept us through the year,
When danger and distress were near.

We pray Thee, O Eternal Son,
Who with the Father reign'st as One,
To guard and rule Thy Christendom
Through all the ages yet to come.

Take not Thy saving Word away,
Our souls' true comfort and their stay;
Abide with us, and keep us free
From errors, following only Thee.

Oh help us to forsake all sin,
A new and holier course begin,
Mark not what once was done amiss,
A happier, better year be this:

Wherein as Christians we may live,
Or die in peace that Thou canst give,
To rise again when Thou shalt come,
And enter Thine eternal home.

There shall we thank Thee, and adore,
With all the angels evermore;
Lord Jesus Christ, increase our faith
To praise Thy name through life and death!

See:
"The Old Year Now Hath Passed Away"
http://www.hymnsandcarolsofchristmas.com/Hymns
_and_Carols/old_year_now_hath_passed_awa.htm

Help Us, O Lord, Behold We Enter

For The New Year

Johann von Rist, 1644

Source: *The Chorale Book For England,* 1863

Help us, O Lord, behold we enter
Upon another year to-day;
In Thee our hopes and thoughts now centre,
Renew our courage for the way:
New life, new strength, new happiness,
We ask of Thee,—oh hear and bless!

May every plan and undertaking
This year be all begun with Thee,
When I am sleeping or am waking,
Still let me know Thou art with me;
Abroad do Thou my footsteps guide,
At home be ever at my side.

Be this a time of grace and pardon,
Thy rod I take with willing mind,
But suffer nought my heart to harden,
Oh let me now Thy mercy find;
In Thee alone, my God, I live,
Thou only canst my sins forgive.

And may this year to me be holy,
Thy grace so fill my ev'ry thought
That all my life be pure and lowly
And truthful, as a Christian's ought;
So make me while yet dwelling here
Pious and blest from year to year.

Jesus, be with me and direct me;
Jesus, my plans and hopes inspire;
Jesus, from tempting thoughts protect me;
Jesus, be all my heart's desire;
Jesus, be in my thoughts all day,
Nor suffer me to fall away!

And grant, Lord, when the year is over,
That it for me in peace may close;
In all things care for me, and cover
My head in time of fear and woes;
So may I, when my years are gone,
Appear with joy before Thy throne.

See:
"Help Us O Lord Behold We Enter"
http://www.hymnsandcarolsofchristmas.com/Hymns
_and_Carols/help_us_o_lord_behold_we_enter.htm

Oh Wouldst Thou
In Thy Glory Come

For The New Year

August Hermann Francke, 1691

Source: _The Chorale Book For England,_ 1863

Oh wouldst Thou in Thy glory come,
As Thou, Lord, hast foretold it!
I count the moment's weary sum
Until we may behold it;
With burning lamp, the Church, Thy Bride,
Is waiting for the holy tide
When Thou, Lord, wilt unfold it.

Yet I would leave it to thy choice,
The hour when we shall meet Thee!
Though Thou dost love that heart and voice
Should daily thus entreat Thee,
And henceforth all my course should be
Still looking on and up to Thee,
With heart prepared to greet Thee.

I joy that from Thy love divine
No power my soul can sever;
That I may dare to call Thee mine,
My Lord, my Friend, for ever!
That I, O Prince of Life, shall be
Made wholly one in heaven with Thee,
In life that endeth never.

And therefore do my thanks o'erflow
That one more year is ended,
And of this Time, so poor, so slow,
Another step ascended;
And with a heart that may not wait
I hasten towards the golden gate
Where long my hopes have tended.

And when the wearied hands give way,
And wearied knees are failing,
Then make Thy mighty arm my stay,
Though faith and hope seem quailing;
That so my heart drink in new strength,
And fear no more the journey's length,
O'er doubt and pain prevailing.

Then on, my soul, with fearless faith,
Let nought to terror move thee,
Nor list what earthly pleasure saith,
When she would lure and prove thee;
The eagles' wings of love and prayer
Will bear thee through life's toil and care
To Him who still doth love thee.

Victorian Visions

See:

"Oh Wouldst Thou In Thy Glory Come"
http://www.hymnsandcarolsofchristmas.com/Hymns
_and_Carols/oh_wouldst_thou_in_thy_glory_com.htm

Poems For The Epiphany

How Brightly Beams The Morning Star

Johann Adolf Schlegel, 1765

Source: *The Chorale Book For England,* 1863

How brightly beams the Morning Star!
What sudden radiance from afar
Doth glad us with its shining,
Brightness of God that breaks our night
And fills the darken'd souls with light
Who long for truth were pining!
Thy Word, Jesu, Only feeds us,
Rightly leads us,
Life bestowing;
Praise, oh praise such love o'erflowing.

Thou here my Comfort, there my Crown,
Thou King of Heaven, who camest down
To dwell as man beside me;
My heart doth praise Thee o'er and o'er,
If Thou art mine I ask no more,
Be wealth or fame denied me;
Thee I seek now; None who proves Thee,
None who loves Thee
Finds Thee fail him;
Lord of life, Thy powers avail him!

Victorian Visions

Through Thee alone can I be blest,
Then deep be on my heart imprest
The love that Thou hast borne me;
So make it ready to fulfil
With burning zeal Thy holy will,
Though men may vex or scorn me;
Saviour, let me Never lose Thee,
For I choose Thee,
Thirst to know Thee;
All I am and have I owe Thee!

O God, our Father far above,
Thee too I Praise, for all the love
Thou in Thy Son dost give me!
In Him am I made one with Thee,
My Brother and my Friend is He;
Shall aught affright or grieve me?
He is Greatest, Best, and Highest,
Ever nighest
To the weakest;
Fear no foes, if Him thou seekest!

O praise to Him who come to save,
Who conquer'd death and burst the grave;
Each day new praise resoundeth
To Him the Lamb who once was slain,
The Friend whom none shall trust in vain,
Whose grace for aye aboundeth;
Sing, ye Heavens, Tell the story
Of His glory,
Till His praises
Flood with light Earth's darkest places.

See:

"How Brightly Beams the Morning Star"
http://www.hymnsandcarolsofchristmas.com/Hymns
_and_Carols/how_brightly_beams_the_morning_s.ht
m

Christ Our Example

Luise Hensel

Source: *Lyra Germanica:* Second Series, The Christian
Life, 1858

E ver would I fain be reading
  In the ancient holy Book,
Of my Saviour's gentle pleading,
  Truth in every word and look.

How when children came He bless'd them,
  Suffer'd no man to reprove,
Took them in His arms, and press'd them
  To His heart with words of love.

How to all the sick and tearful
  Help was ever gladly shown;
How He sought the poor and fearful,
  Call'd them brothers and His own.

How no contrite soul e'er sought Him,
  And was bidden to depart,
How with gentle words He taught him,
  Took the death from out his heart.

Still I read the ancient story,
  And my joy is ever new,
How for us He left His glory,
  How He still is kind and true.

How the flock He gently leadeth
  Whom His Father gave Him here;
How His arms He widely spreadeth
  To His heart to draw us near.

Catherine Winkworth

Let me kneel, my Lord, before Thee,
   Let my heart in tears o'erflow,
Melted by Thy love adore Thee,
   Blest in Thee 'mid joy or woe!

Forsaking All For The True Light

Laurentius Laurenti, 1700

Source: *Lyra Germanica:* Second Series, The Christian
Life, 1858

I s thy heart athirst to know
   That the King of heaven and earth
Deigns to dwell with man below,
   Yea hath stoop'd to mortal birth?
Search the Word with ceaseless care
Till thou find this treasure there.

With the sages from afar
   Journey on o'er sea and land,
Till thou see the Morning Star
   O'er thy heart unchanging stand,
Then shalt thou behold His face
Full of mercy, truth and grace.

For if Christ be born within,
   Soon that likeness shall appear
Which the heart had lost through sin,
   God's own image fair and clear,
And the soul serene and bright
Mirrors back His heavenly light.

Jesus, let me seek for nought,
But that Thou shouldst dwell in me;
Let this only fill my thought,
How I may grow liker Thee,
Through this early care and strife,
Through the calm eternal life.

With the wise who know Thee right,
Though the world accounts them fools,
I will praise Thee day and night,
I will order by Thy rules
All my life, that it may be
Fill'd with praise and love of Thee.

Note:

Also found in Catherine Winkworth, *The Chorale Book For England*, 1863. See: "Is Thy Heart Athirst To Know."
http://www.hymnsandcarolsofchristmas.com/Hymns_and_Carols/is_thy_heart_athirst_to_know.htm

O Jesu, King of Glory

Martin Behemb (Behm, Böhme), 1606

Source: *The Chorale Book For England,* 1863

O Jesu, King of Glory!
Our Sov'reign and our Friend!
Thy throne is fix'd in Heaven,
Thy kingdom hath no end:
Oh now to all men, far and near,
Lord, make it known, we pray,
That as in Heaven all creatures here
May know Thee and obey.

The Eastern sages bringing
Their tribute-gifts to Thee,
Bear witness to Thy Kingdom,
And humbly bow the knee;
To Thee the Morning Star doth lead,
To Thee th' inspired Word,
We hail Thee, Saviour in our need,
We worship Thee, the Lord.

Ah, look on me with pity,
Though I am weak and poor,
Admit me to Thy kingdom
To dwell there blest and sure.
Oh rescue me from all my woes,
And shield me with Thine arm
From Sin and Death, the mighty foes
That daily seek our harm.

And bid Thy Word within us
Shine as the fairest Star;
Keep sin and all false doctrine
From all Thy people far:
Let us Thy name aright confess,
And with Thy Christendom,
Our King and Saviour own and bless
Through all the world to come.

See:
"O Jesu, King of Glory"
http://www.hymnsandcarolsofchristmas.com/Hymns
and_Carols/o_jesu_king_of_glory.htm

Rise, O Salem, Rise And Shine

Johann von Rist, 1655

Source: _The Chorale Book For England,_ 1863

Rise, O Salem, rise and shine!
Lo! the Gentiles hail thy waking;
Herald of a morn divine,
See the dayspring o'er us breaking,
Telling God has call'd to mind
Those who long in darkness pined.

Ah, how blindly did we stray,
Ere this sun our earth had brightened,
Heaven we sought not, for no ray
Had our 'wilder'd eyes enlighten'd!
All our looks were earthward bent,
All our strength on earth was spent.

But, the day-spring from on high
Hath arisen with beams unclouded,
And we all before it fly
All the heavy gloom that shrouded
This sad earth, where sin and woe
Seem'd to reign o'er all below.

Thy appearing, Lord, shall fill
All my thoughts in sorrow's hour;
Thy appearing, Lord, shall still
All my dread of death's dark power;
Whether joy or tears be mine,
Through them still Thy light shall shine.

Let me, when my course is run,
Calmly leave a world of sadness
For the place that needs no sun,
For Thou art its light and gladness,
For the mansions fair and bright,
Where Thy saints are crown'd with light.

See:
    "Rise, O Salem, Rise And Shine"
http://www.hymnsandcarolsofchristmas.com/Hymns
_and_Carols/rise_o_salem_rise_and_shine.htm

The King of Men

Martin Behemb (Behm, Böhme), 1616

Source: *Lyra Germanica:* Second Series, The Christian
Life, 1858

O King of Glory! David's Son!
   Our Sovereign and our Friend!
In Heaven for ever stands Thy throne,
   Thy kingdom hath no end:
Oh now to all men, far and near,
   Lord, make it known, we pray,
That as in heaven all creatures here
   May know Thee and obey.

The Eastern sages gladly bring
   Their tribute-gifts to Thee;
They witness that Thou art their King,
   And humbly bow the knee;
To Thee the Morning Star doth lead,
   To Thee th' inspired Word,
We hail Thee, Saviour in our need,
   We worship Thee, the Lord.

Ah look on me with pitying grace,
   Though weak and poor I be,
Within Thy kingdom grant a place
   Secure and blest to me.
Oh rescue me from all my woes,
   And shield me with Thine arm
From Sin and Death, the mighty foes
   That daily seek our harm.

And bid Thy Word, the fairest Star,
   Within us clearly shine;
Keep sin and all false doctrine far,
   Since Thou hast claim'd us Thine:
Let us Thy name aright confess,
   And with Thy Christendom,
Our King and Saviour own and bless
   Through all the world to come.

The Light of the World

Johann Heerman, 1630

Source: *Lyra Germanica:* Second Series, The Christian Life, 1858

O Christ, our true and only Light
Illuminate Those who sit in night,
Let those afar now hear Thy voice,
And in Thy fold with us rejoice.

Fill with the radiance of Thy grace
The souls now lost in error's maze,
And all who in their secret minds
Some dark delusion hurts and blinds.

And all who else have stray'd from Thee,
O gently seek! Thy healing be
To every wounded conscience given,
And let them also share Thy heaven.

Oh make the deaf to hear Thy word,
And teach the dumb to speak, dear Lord,
Who dare not yet the faith avow,
Though secretly they hold it now.

Shine on the darken'd and the cold,
Recall the wanderers from Thy fold,
Unit those now who walk apart,
Confirm the weak and doubting heart.

So they with us may evermore
Such grace with wondering thanks adore,
And endless praise to Thee be given
By all Thy Church in earth and heaven.

The Manifestation
of the Light of the World

Johann von Rist, 1655

Source: *Lyra Germanica:* First Series, Songs for the
Household, 1855

*Arise, shine, for thy light is come, and the glory of the
Lord is risen upon thee!*

From the Lesson

All ye Gentile lands awake!
    Thou, O Salem, rise and shine!
See the day-spring o'er you break,
    Heralding a morn divine,
Telling, God hath call'd to mind
Those who long in darkness pined.

Lo! the shadows flee away,
    For our Light is come at length,
Brighter than all earthly day,
    Source of being, life, and strength!
Whoso on this Light would gaze
Must forsake all evil ways.

Ah how blindly did we stray
    Ere shone forth this glorious Sun,
Seeking each his separate way,
    Leaving Heaven, unsought, unwon;
All our looks were earthward bent,
All our strength on earth was spend.

Earthly were our thoughts and low,
  In the toils of Folly caught,
Toss'd of Satan to and fro,
  Counting goodness all for nought;
By the world and flesh deceived,
Heaven's true joys we disbelieved.

Then were hidden from our eyes
  All the law and grace of God;
Rich and poor, the fools and wise,
  Wanting light to find the road
Leading to the heavenly life,
Wander'd lost in care and strife.

But the glory of the Lord
  Hath arisen on us to-day,
We have seen the light outpour'd
  That must surely drive away
All things that to night belong,
All the sad earth's woe and wrong.

Thy arising, Lord, shall fill
  All my thoughts in sorrow's hour;
Thy arising, Lord, shall still
  All my dread of Death's dark power:
Through my smiles and through my tears
Still Thy light, O Lord, appears.

Let me, Lord, in peace depart
  From this evil world to Thee;
Where Thyself sole Brightness art,
  Thou hast kept a place for me:
In the shining city there
Crowns of light Thy saints shall wear.

Poems For The Presentation In The Temple

Light Of The Gentile Nations

Johann Franck (Frank), 1653

Source: *The Chorale Book For England,* 1863

L ight of the Gentile nations,
    Thy people's joy and love,
Dawn by Thy Spirit hither,
    We gladly come to prove
Thy presence in Thy temple,
    And wait with earnest mind,
As Simeon once had waited
    His Saviour God to find.

Yes, Lord, Thy servants meet Thee,
    Ev'n now, in ev'ry place,
Where Thy true word hath promised
    That they should see Thy face.
Thou yet wilt gently grant us,
    Who gather round Thee here,
In faith's strong arms to bear Thee,
    As once that aged seer.

Be Thou our joy, our brightness,
  That shines 'mid pain and loss,
Our Sun in times of terror,
  The glory round our cross;
A glow in sinking spirits,
  A sunbeam in distress,
Physician, friend in sickness;
  In death our happiness.

Let us, O Lord, be faithful
  With Simeon to the end,
That so his dying song may
  From all our hearts ascend;
"O Lord, now let Thy servant
  Depart in peace for aye,
Since I have seen my Saviour,
  Have here beheld His day."

My Saviour, I behold Thee
  Now with the eye of faith;
No foe of Thee can rob me,
  Though bitter words he saith;
Within Thy heart abiding,
  As Thou dost dwell in me,
No pain, no death has terrors
  To part my soul from Thee!

See:

"Light Of The Gentile Nations"
http://www.hymnsandcarolsofchristmas.com/Hymns
 and Carols/light of the gentile nations.htm

In Peace And Joy I Now Depart

Martin Luther, 1525

Source: *The Chorale Book For England,* 1863

In peace and joy I now depart,
According to God's will,
For full of comfort is my heart,
So calm and sweet and still;
So doth God His promise keep,
And death for me is but a sleep.

'T is Christ hath wrought this work for me,
Thy dear and only son,
Whom Thou hast suffer'd me to see,
And made Him surely known
As my Help when trouble's rife,
And even in death itself my Life.

For Thou In mercy unto all
Hast set this Saviour forth;
And to His kingdom Thou dost call
The nations of the earth
Through His blessed wholesome Word,
That now in every place is heard.

He is the heathens' saving Light,
And He will gently lead
Those who now know Thee not aright,
And in His pastures feed;
While His people's joy He is,
Their Sun, their glory, and their bliss.

See:
  "In Peace And Joy I Now Depart"
http://www.hymnsandcarolsofchristmas.com/Hymns
_and_Carols/in_peace_and_joy_i_now_depart.htm

Here Ends

The Christmas Poems
Of
Catherine Winkworth

Victorian Visions

Sources

Katherine Lee Bates. *America The Beautiful And Other Poems*. New York: Thomas Y. Crowell Company, 1911.

Katherine Lee Bates. *Fairy Gold*. New York: E. P. Dutton & Co., 1916.

Katherine Lee Bates. *Sunshine And Other Verses For Children*. "Printed by the Wellesley Alumnæ for the Benefit of the Norumbega Fund 1890."

Katherine Lee Bates. *The Retinue And Other Poems*. New York: E. P. Dutton & Co., 1918.

Mackenzie Bell. *Christina Rossetti: A Biographical and Critical Study*. Boston: Roberts Brothers, 1898.

William Sterndale Bennett and Otto Goldschmidt, eds. *The Chorale Book For England*. The Hymns from the Lyra Germanica and Other Sources, Translated by Catherine Winkworth. London: Longman, Green, Longman, Roberts, and Green, 1863.

Louis F. Benson. *Studies of Familiar Hymns, First Series*. Philadelphia: The Westminster Press, 1924.

Dorothy Burgess. *Dream and Deed: The Story of Katharine Lee Bates*. Norman: University of Oklahoma Press, 1952.

Rev. Duncan Campbell. *Hymns and Hymn Makers*. London: A & C. Black, 1908.

David Chalkley. The Havergal Trust; http://www.havergaltrust.com/index.html ;

Biographical note concerning Frances Havergal: http://www.havergaltrust.com/frhavergal.html. Accessed May 26, 2007.

Christian Classics Ethereal Library. Additional information from a biographical note about Catherine Winkworth which was appended to a later version (Second Edition, 1961) of *Lyra Germanica* by a niece. See generally http://www.ccel.org/w/winkworth/

Martha Foote Crow, ed. *Christ In The Poetry Of Today.* New York: The Womans Press, 1917.

R. [Rebecca] W. Crump, ed. *The Complete Poems of Christina Rossetti,* Vol. 3. Penguin, 2001.

Emily E.S. Elliott. *Chimes of Consecration.* London: Seeley, Jackson, and Halliday, 1875.

"Emily Elizabeth Steele Elliott." *Cyberhymnal,* citing Charles S. Nutter and Wilbur F. Tillett, The *Hymns and Hymn Writers of the Church.* New York: The Methodist Book Concern, 1911; http://www.cyberhymnal.org/bio/e/l/elliott_ees.htm

O. Hardwig, ed. *Wartburg Hymnal.* Chicago: Wartburg Publishing House, 1918.

"Frances Ridley Havergal."*Cyberhymnal.* http://www.cyberhymnal.org/bio/h/a/v/havergal_fr. htm

"Frances Ridley Havergal." *Hymnuts.* http://hymnuts.luthersem.edu/hcompan/writers/fh avrgal.htm

Maria V. G. Havergal, ed. *The Poetical Works of Frances Ridley Havergal.* Toronto: Toronto Williard Tract Depot, No Date (circa 1880, 855 pages).

William Hone. *Ancient Mysteries Described*. London: 1823.

Rev. Charles Lewis Hutchins, ed. *Carols Old and Carols New*. Boston: Parish Choir, 1916.

John Julian. *Dictionary of Hymnology*. 1892, Second Ed., 1907; republished by Dover Editions in 1957 in two volumes.

J. F. Kinsey and John McPherson, eds. *Echoes Of Glory For The Sunday School*. LaFayette, Indiana: The Echo Music Company, 1888.

J. Foster Kirk., ed. *Allibone's Dictionary of English Literature and British And American Authors*. Supplement. Philadelphia: JB Lippincott Co., 1891.

Robert Guy McCutchan. *Our Hymnody: A Manual of the Methodist Church*. Second Edition. New York: Abingdon Press, 1937.

W. H. Monk and C. Steggall, eds. *Hymns Ancient and Modern*. London, William Clowes and Sons, Old Edition, 1889.

The Parish School Hymnal. Philadelphia: Board of Publication of the United Lutheran Church in America, 1926.

Christina Rossetti. *Poems By Christiana Rossetti*. Boston: Brown, Little and Company, 1906; Project Gutenberg EBook #19188.

Christina Rossetti. *Goblin Market, The Prince's Progress, and Other Poems*, World's Classics, 1913; Project Gutenberg EBook #16950.

William Michael Rossetti, ed. *The Poetical Works of Christina Georgina Rossetti, with a Memoir and Notes.* London: Macmillan And Co., Limited, 1904.

Robert Haven Schauffler, ed. *Christmas: Its Origin, Celebration and Significance as Related in Prose and Verse.* 1907.

Dorothy Middlebrook Shipman, ed. *Stardust & Holly.* New York: The Macmillan Co., 1933.

Leslie Stephen, ed. *Dictionary of National Biography.* Vol. XVII. New York: Macmillan and Co., 1889.

Catherine Winkworth. *Christian Singers Of Germany.* 1869.

"Catherine Winkworth." *Cyberhymnal.* http://www.cyberhymnal.org/bio/w/i/n/winkworth_c.htm

"Catherine Winkworth." *Hymnuts.* http://hymnuts.luthersem.edu/hcompan/writers/wnkwrth.htm

Catherine Winkworth. *Lyra Germanica, First Series: Songs of the Household.* London: G. Routledge, 1855.

Catherine Winkworth. *Lyra Germanica, Second Series: The Christian Life.* London: Longman, Green, Longman, and Roberts, 1858.

Index Of First Lines

Christmas Volumes

Edited by Douglas D. Anderson

Novel Format
6" x 9"

Victorian Visions
A Christmas Poetry Collection
Paperback: http://www.lulu.com/content/1057593
Hardcover With Dust Jacket:
http://www.lulu.com/content/1102962
Glossy Hardback: http://www.lulu.com/content/1103006

Divinely Inspired
A Christmas Poetry Collection
Paperback: http://www.lulu.com/content/1057550
Hardcover With Dust Jacket:
http://www.lulu.com/content/1103033
Glossy Hardback: http://www.lulu.com/content/1103051

The Bridegroom Cometh
Poetry for the Advent
Coming Soon!

Large Page Format
8 ½" x 11"

So Gracious Is The Time
A Christmas Poetry Collection
Volume 1
Paperback: http://www.lulu.com/content/871615
Glossy Hardback: http://www.lulu.com/content/997838

Once A Lovely Shining Star
A Christmas Poetry Collection
Volume 2
Paperback: http://www.lulu.com/content/945653
Glossy Hardback: http://www.lulu.com/content/998039

How Still The Night
The Christmas Poems of Father Andrew, S.D.C.
Paperback: http://www.lulu.com/content/911838
Glossy Hardback: http://www.lulu.com/content/998000

Father *AND* Daughter
Christmas Poems by William Henry Havergal
and Frances Ridley Havergal
Paperback: http://www.lulu.com/content/909456
Glossy Hardback: http://www.lulu.com/content/997975

Now, Now Comes The Mirth
Christmas Poetry by Robert Herrick
Paperback: http://www.lulu.com/content/871847
Glossy Hardback: http://www.lulu.com/content/997910

What Sudden Blaze Of Song
The Christmas Poems of John Keble
Paperback: http://www.lulu.com/content/918619
Glossy Hardback: http://www.lulu.com/content/998014

A Holy Heavenly Chime
The Christmastide Poems of Christiana Georgina Rossetti
Paperback: http://www.lulu.com/content/871797
Glossy Hardback: http://www.lulu.com/content/997900

All My Heart This Night Rejoices
The Christmas Poems of Catherine Winkworth
Paperback: http://www.lulu.com/content/871714
Glossy Hardback: http://www.lulu.com/content/997889

A Victorian Carol Book
Favorite carols from the 19th Century.
Spiral-bound Paperback: http://www.lulu.com/content/133804
Paperback: http://www.lulu.com/content/1048777
Glossy Hardback: http://www.lulu.com/content/997946

Douglas Anderson's Christmas Storefront
http://stores.lulu.com/carols_book

All Volumes Printed by
Lulu, Inc.
Morrisville, North Carolina 27560
www.lulu.com

The Hymns And Carols Of Christmas
www.HymnsAndCarolsOfChristmas.com

Over 2,800 Christmas hymns and carols,
plus a large number of Christmas poems and prose.

*Proceeds from the sale of these books
help support this web site.
Thank-you.*

www.ingramcontent.com/pod-product-compliance
Lightning Source LLC
Chambersburg PA
CBHW030412100426
42812CB00028B/2927/J